Praise for
You're Leaving When?

A *Good Morning America* Must-Read Book of the Month

"In her new collection of essays, *You're Leaving When?: Adventures in Downward Mobility*, [Annabelle Gurwitch] writes with hilarious poignancy about tackling midlife malaise on an austerity budget." —*Los Angeles Magazine*

"[Gurwitch] trains a skeptical eye on her era's foibles in the manner of a Dorothy Parker, leavens it with the housefrau elan of an Erma Bombeck, and spices it with her own witty, irrepressible personality."
—BILL THOMPSON, *The Post and Courier*

"*You're Leaving When?* will most likely feel like a long, intimate chat with your funniest friend." —SAMANTHA SCHOECH, *San Francisco Chronicle*

"Annabelle Gurwitch is wry, witty, and a master of the bon mot."
—DIANA WAGMAN, *Alta*

"Erma Bombeck meets Dorothy Parker in this topical and often laugh-out-loud funny take on our modern malaise." —*Kirkus Reviews*

"By turns bittersweet and hilarious." —*Publishers Weekly*

"The latest from Gurwitch will have readers rolling with laughter one minute and picking up the phone to commiserate with friends or family the next. Gurwitch's perspective on both the major and the mundane will be relatable to anyone who understands how the American Dream has devolved into a fever dream." —*Library Journal*

"Thoroughly modern and thoroughly entertaining." —*PureWow*

You're Leaving When?

You're Leaving When?

ADVENTURES IN DOWNWARD MOBILITY

ANNABELLE GURWITCH

COUNTERPOINT
Berkeley, California

You're Leaving When?

The Library of Congress has cataloged the hardcover as follows:

Names: Gurwitch, Annabelle, author.
Title: You're leaving when? : adventures in downward mobility / Annabelle
   Gurwitch.
Other titles: You are leaving when
Description: First hardcover edition | Berkeley, California : Counterpoint,
   [2021] | Includes bibliographical references.
Identifiers: LCCN 2020030991 | ISBN 9781640094475 (hardcover) | ISBN
   9781640094482 (ebook)
Subjects: LCSH: Middle-aged mothers—Humor. | Mothers and sons—Humor. |
   Gender-nonconforming children—Humor. | Downward mobility (Social
   sciences)—Humor.
Classification: LCC HQ759.43 .G87 2021 | DDC 306.874/30844--dc23
LC record available at https://lccn.loc.gov/2020030991

Paperback ISBN: 978-1-64009-527-4

Cover design by Jenny Carrow and Dana Li
Book design by Jordan Koluch

COUNTERPOINT
2560 Ninth Street, Suite 318
Berkeley, CA 94710
www.counterpointpress.com

Printed in the United States of America

10 9 8 7 6 5 4 3 2 1

For Ezra
there will always be a toothbrush
and a life-size sarcophagus waiting for you at home

Contents

You're Leaving When?

I Thought There'd Be Coasting

IT WAS THE WORST OF times, it was the worst of times.

My friend Sasha and I are meeting up for an impromptu lunch. Sasha proposed a casual Mediterranean café on the east side of Los Angeles, the kind of place where you order from the counter and a server drops it off at your table. It's not an expensive eatery, but I'm on my recently instituted austerity budget, so I scarf down a few handfuls of almonds on the ride over and order a small side of pickled radishes. Sasha gets a lamb kebab salad, and had I known she was picking up the check, I would have ordered that too. Drizzled with creamy tahini dressing, it looks and smells delicious. When she invites me to tuck into it, I accept with an amount of enthusiasm that startles both of us. "Thank you," I gush as though I hadn't eaten in weeks, which is not true. If anything, I've been stress eating; it's just that lately even small gestures of kindness seem as precious as winning the lottery.

Sasha and I have only been in sporadic touch over the last few eventful years, and as we catch up she tells me that she has just enrolled her family in Medi-Cal, our state-sponsored low-income health insurance plan. I'm stunned. She always seems so . . . so . . . downright jaunty, at least on social media. But no, we're in similar straits, like ducks, madly paddling just below the surface.

Much of her regular employment has evaporated—her income, like mine, is now subject to the vagaries of the gig economy. Decades of maintaining a manageable if sometime marginal stability have imploded, sending us on a roller coaster of emotional and financial mobility, a decidedly downhill ride.

I explain that I recently lost my coveted union health insurance and am considering following the lead of a friend who'd recently signed up for an absurdly affordable plan, the only catch being that you had to have a preexisting condition. "What is it? I might already have it," Sasha said, hopeful at the prospect of lowering her overhead even more.

"Accepting Jesus Christ as your savior. Oh, and they don't cover birth control," I answer. And that's when we lose it, dissolving into a fit of laughter because we're both in menopause and birth control is one of the only things we no longer have to worry about.

After inhaling most of her kebab, I treat us to coffee; we share a cookie and commiserate. We are not living in a war zone; we are not economic or climate refugees. We are so fortunate. As we say goodbye, the last bite of cookie wrapped in a napkin in my purse, we hug, clinging to each other longer than either of us expected. When did things go so horribly wrong?

THIS IS HOW IT STARTED.

In the weeks before my kid flew the coop, I was racing around the house like a maniac.

"You need to know how to boil an egg! Iron a shirt! Make a fire by rubbing two sticks together!"

"Mom, I'm vegan. I'll be living in a dorm, you don't know how to start a fire without matches, and nobody irons anymore. We don't even own an iron."

From what I'd read, after our tearful college dorm room good-byes, my future would be filled with hot-air balloon tours and Zumba classes. Motherhood? My work was done. Kid successfully launched, with all that me-time, I could improve the quality of my life, enjoy my blissfully quiet and tidy home. Maybe I'd learn to make soup from scratch; my husband and I would rekindle our waning desire for each other. Not only that, I was excitedly planning on replacing the living room sofa we'd had since before we'd gotten married, twenty years prior.

That love seat had seen a lot of action. It was the first piece of furniture we'd bought together and it was perfect for newlywed canoodling. Then came baby puke, mac and cheese spillage, popcorn grease, and pen marks, followed by teenage hormones. A friend of Ezra's had camped out on the couch for a week, that last hurrah before heading off to college. Echo had some kind of endocrine disorder, and now I couldn't get the scent of armpits and old sneakers out of the fabric. After my kid was safely ensconced in their college dorm room, I went furniture shopping at a neighborhood store. It's the kind of place that sells handmade chocolates and candles with ironically themed scents like "neo-hippie bullshit" and "nonbinary anxiety," and carries a furniture line named for iconic Californian authors. The James Ellroy: louche, low to the ground, ideal landing spot for the falling down drunk. The Bukowski: a bit hulking, large enough to accommodate a big man or a couple in flagrante. The

Didion: half the size, more delicately rendered, nothing froufrou about it. I was leaning Bukowski. I had plans for that couch. Sure, my marriage had been so strained we'd been sleeping in separate bedrooms for upward of a year, but in the 1950s, couples spent entire marriages in separate bedrooms.

The state of our union wasn't perfect. I assumed my husband and I weren't any more miserable than everyone else who made the same amount of money as we did. I'd see him passed out on the couch, frustrated by the transactional nature of our relationship, and I'd wonder: was it worth it to forgo garlic for dinner (bloating, so unattractive) and persevere in the search for the perfect lube (chafing, so excruciating)? If we could just muddle through these middling years, I calculated that between Social Security and our union pensions, we could look forward to a moderate but reliable income when we turned sixty-five. Provided Social Security remained solvent. Provided our union pension plan didn't implode. Provided I could keep providing an income, as I was the breadwinner at that point. That was a lot of providers, but I was counting on them.

I was holding up a selection of swatches when my husband announced that I should pick out the fabric I liked best. He, too, had plans. They just didn't include me. Instead of a new couch, he wanted a new life.

Then both of my parents died; my kid landed in rehab for drug and alcohol addiction; failing to qualify for my union's health insurance meant the family premium ballooned, leaving my finances in further disarray; one of my cats disappeared; and my tennis teacher fired me.

Getting booted from my weekly cardio tennis class, at twenty dollars a pop, seemed like a low blow. Sure, I was showing up late, without sneakers, and weeping continuously throughout the lesson, but the six other mothers and I had been playing since our kids were in middle school together, and this was my last connection to that parent community. Despite five years of lessons, I'd dubbed my serve "the matzoh ball," because although it looks like it's got substance, it crumbles on impact. I wore my lack of improvement as a badge of honor. I was reliably inept. In a world that was constantly changing, at least I was consistent.

I began having a traffic-related fantasy. I've obviously lived in Los Angeles way too long, because traffic has seeped into every part of my imagination. In this scenario, the car traveling behind me stops so close to my rear fender, it almost bumps into me. I get out of my vehicle, sashay over, and politely explain to the driver, "You know, friend, you really shouldn't do that, it's not neighborly and someone could get hurt. Have a great day. Peace out!" The driver takes out a gun and shoots me. I expire right there at the intersection of Bright Lights and Broken Dreams. I die happy because I was right and I was nice about it.

With any luck, I'd go instantly—with my new health insurance, I couldn't afford a slow decline.

I was keenly aware that I had nowhere near the challenges facing millions of people around the globe. That I was well aware of this only made me feel worse. To feel immobilized when perfectly aware of your privilege made death by inconsequential traffic incident seem even more desirable.

"You need to embrace this next chapter," my friend Tonya insisted.

So did my accountant.

"Don't next-chapter me," I told them. "Next chapter is spin for 'dreaded challenges you're about to encounter on your journey' and should be as suspect as someone telling you 'having cancer can be a gift.'" I'm fifty-five. Is there anyone who's thrilled about starting a next chapter at my age? When does the coasting begin? I thought I'd be coasting by now.

Something had to give. Or rather, everything had to give.

It wasn't a shock to read that the rate of people in my age range filing for bankruptcy is three times what it was in 1991. One-third reported that helping aging parents and children, coupled with rising health-care costs, were contributing factors. Others were bumping up against that gray ceiling in their chosen fields and pursuing new endeavors or going back to school.

There is no upside to downward financial mobility, but there is value in reassessing priorities. Indulging in even a modicum of retail therapy or taking that island vacation to regain your mojo are other midlife rites of passage that have fallen by the wayside. I'd hoped to one day get my kitchen remodeled; instead, I had my vagina reupholstered.

Even friends who'd managed financial solvency were dealing with the emotional stresses of our Gen Z offspring. Our children no longer go off to college and set up shop in some city or town, returning home only for vacations or holidays. No, they come back to the childhood bedrooms they grew up in. My neighbor's son came home for a gap year that lasted for three. Remember when the phrase "eighteen and out" was a familiar refrain? Pew Research reports that, for the first time in 130 years, a third of young adults in America are living with their parents.

My friend Paula's story is a cautionary tale. After sending her youngest off to college, she celebrated. *Kids launched*: check that off the to-do list. She'd downsized from her spacious but pricey two bedroom to a modest one bedroom/one bathroom in Manhattan when she received a notification that her son's college dorm fee was doubling. He attends school locally, so they converted a walk-in closet in her living room into a bedroom for him. Then her daughter, a recent college grad who was living with her father in California, decided she wanted to give it a go in New York. With her son in a closet and her daughter on her couch, Paula is tithing her income to a Reiki practitioner. As Paula says, "It's hard to know what to expect. I'm not sure when they'll ever move out."

My kid entered college a music major. Every parent knows that's tantamount to announcing, "My future plans include living in my parents' basement."

I also lost a son, but gained a gender nonbinary kid. The summer that Ezra got sober, they began identifying as a grammar-defying queer person, and I began relearning my pronouns one day at a time. To honor their gender expression, I write about my child in these stories using the pronouns they, them, theirs.

To remain in the family home in anticipation of my kid's return, my nest, by necessity, has been monetized. I joined the legions pioneering new iterations of old-world home sharing. Barely a week goes by without an item in the news touting home sharing's benefits, including preventing loneliness and isolation. Here's a scene I never pictured for myself in my fifties: wondering if the couple with tattoos, one reading GRIFTER and the other DRIFTER, would make for good roomies.

Where we once expected to sprint to the launch of the offspring, midlife parenting is now, more than ever, an endurance sport, a marathon with no finish line in sight. All speculation aside over whether helicopter parenting or snowplow parenting or even combine harvester parenting (OK, I made that one up) is to blame, the net effect is that parents of adult children can find that they are— still—always on call. Along with the expected "send money," if you are the parent of a child born between 1990 and this morning, I can almost guarantee that you'll receive this text: "When a piercing gets infected, what should you put on it?" I didn't even know my child had a piercing. Or five. I'm going to save you the trouble of googling the answer: it's saline solution.

I WROTE THE LAST CHAPTERS of this book as people across the globe endured incalculable losses in the wake of COVID-19. In my little corner of the world, Ezra completed their last semester of college online, officially earning a BA in music, although arguably the last months were spent majoring in Rubik's Cube and minoring in sourdough starter. Their college graduation speaker was supposed to be David Byrne. Instead, as Ezra sheltered in place on campus, I watched a truncated, livestreamed ceremony alone in my backyard. Names silently scrolled by on the tiny screen; even the font was unremarkable.

The need to cultivate adaptability in the face of an unknown future, even more pressing than when I started writing the stories in this collection, made me look to a species that is in many ways our better.

Fifty million years ago, ancient whales, once terrestrial mammals, bid farewell to terra firma and took to the seas. The presence of vestigial limbs can still be seen in modern-day whale flippers. I hope it doesn't come to that, though I won't be surprised if one day I wake up and discover that my newly acquired love handles have morphed into fins. I'm still above water, and that feels like a tiny victory.

Oh, and I did get a new couch. I hope it's well made because it will need to last a long time. I couldn't afford the Didion, the Bukowski, or the Ellroy, but remember Mary's best friend on *The Mary Tyler Moore Show*? Even watching as a kid, I instinctively related to her BFF more than goody-two-shoes, perfectly coiffed Mary. She had career highs and lows, husbands and lovers who came and went, but she survived—even thrived—based on sheer willpower, tenacity, and her unfailing sense of humor. Where Mary could be resistant to change, she rolled with the punches, and while Mary was the straight man (in unfortunate comedy lingo), she got the punch lines. My new couch is kind of the best friend of those superstar sofas.

I call it the Rhoda.

Homeward Bound

"HOMEWARD BOUND," THE SIMON AND Garfunkel megahit, played so often during the time when my brain was the most elastic that the lyrics sometimes float through my head, as though I'd written them myself. In a nutshell, there's this guy who's playing one-night stands and he's pining to go home. I can relate. Whether I've been out of town or out doing errands, there's always that moment when an almost primal urge to return home kicks in.

When friends and family learned that my two-decade marriage was ending, many were at a loss as to how to respond. Was this good news or bad news? "Condolulations" was the terrifically apt neologism coined by my friend Meghan, but "Are you staying in the house?" was often the first question.

Owning a home in Los Angeles is a dicey proposition under any circumstances. Seismologists predict a 99.7 percent chance of a 6.7 magnitude earthquake or larger before 2037. That sentence alone should send people packing. Over the last year, we've experienced record-breaking droughts, heat waves, floods, wildfires, and mudslides. Our weather forecasts should simply read: "Biblical." At my house, the roots of a maple tree interfere with the plumbing. When you take a shower or flush a toilet, it sounds like the percussion section of a middle school jazz band is warming up inside the walls. I can never remember which is the bad kind of cracks, vertical or horizontal, but it doesn't matter, because the walls in the stairwell have both! The settling requires me to hang pictures at an angle to make the sloping floors look less noticeable. Still, every time I open the front door to my home that lists only slightly easterly, I experience that same comforting feeling of slipping into my favorite pair of jeans.

I picked this house out. Actually, I stalked it. I was four months pregnant when I was tasked with finding a home. My ex was out of town working on a television series. One Sunday, the realtor pulled up in front of a 1932 aspirationally colonial stucco. There was nothing extraordinary about the place, no turrets, no whimsical flourishes. In dire need of landscaping, the house had a wood-shingled roof that looked like kindling. Still, in a funky neighborhood at the base of Griffith Park, the largest urban wilderness area in the United States, slopes visible in the near distance, it looked homey.

"The McGarrys, a sweet couple in their nineties, live here," the realtor said. "Mr. McGarry is ill, and when he passes, they'll put it on the market."

"That's my house. I'll wait," I announced on the spot.

It was not a rational decision. But that's how it is when you fall in love. I had the same feeling when I just had to marry "that" guy. Both times.

I was five months pregnant when Mr. McGarry passed and I entered my house for the first time. At about two thousand square feet, the interior was markedly smaller than the exterior had led me to believe, a phenomenon that every single person who has ever visited remarks upon. The walls were nicotine stained and the carpets were dingy, but with pregnancy hormones coursing through my veins, I knew I could transform it into a comfortable nest. It might seem a bad portent to purchase a home where someone had so recently died, but the Widow McGarry was planted on a settee in the living room, cheerfully smoking a cigarette and sipping a martini. It was three o'clock on a Tuesday afternoon. I took that as a good sign. We made an offer.

Geological survey? "Waste of money," said my realtor, correctly sizing me up as a first-time buyer, too intimidated and too pregnant to concern herself with such details.

My house, which, I learned 15 years later, is situated directly over an earthquake fault line, turned out not to be built on granite like the majority of the homes in the area, but on the unstable dirt fill that was excavated when the homes across the street went up. When the Big One hits, it's going to be a rollicking ride.

Still, my child grew up in this house, it's the last of my homes that my parents will have visited, and it's where my ex-husband and I spent many happy hours hate-watching TV shows, the last shared pleasure of a marriage in decline.

To the untrained eye, the backyard is a square of patchy grass, but if you look closely, you can just make out baseball-diamond grooves in the topography that my kid and I carved during thousands of hours of kickball. Later, I passed almost as much time secreted deep in the warren of master bedroom closets, perched on my earthquake to-go bag, keeping an eye on Ezra's backyard teen-age ragers.

On a purely practical level, downsizing wasn't ideal. Even add-ing in the mortgage, insurance, and property taxes, the monthly cost was still lower than the average two-bedroom apartment in town. While we'd accrued a good amount of equity, it wouldn't be nearly enough, after splitting the profit from a sale, for either of us to afford a rental large enough to accommodate our kid's regular visits and potential boomeranging without draining our savings.

Carla's kid is also a musician. His synth-punk-meets-hoedown-inspired band plays local clubs. They're a bunch of clowns. Liter-ally. The band members play in costume and under nom de clowns. Each lives with their parents and juggles a variety of service indus-try gigs. Carla's not sure he'll ever move out. Even the most optimis-tic would be ill advised not to take notice of her friend who seemed to be walking the same path.

I committed to maintaining the family residence, but to do that, I'd need to buy out a portion of my ex's share of the value, and I could only do that by refinancing the mortgage or winning the lottery.

If you've ever refinanced a home, you know that assembling the paperwork seems like a Kafkaesque task designed to weed out people who aren't good at sudoku and ensure that you never read the fine print on the documents you're signing. On that day when a representative from the bank shows up at my door with a cooler and demands the pancreas I agreed to provide as collateral, I won't be a bit surprised. Even with our combined incomes, loan approval was unlikely.

"What will you be using the money for?" asked Grace, our loan officer, as my husband and I nervously held hands in her cubicle in an effort to appear like a couple who were not imminently divorcing.

"Kitchen/bathroom remodel," we answered at the exact same time. "We don't know, maybe both." I giggled. "We also have a big backyard and we're thinking of putting in a pool. Or solar. Solar is so important."

Grace betrayed no emotion as I gave the least convincing performance of my life. I bet she's a kick-ass poker player. Loan approval limbo stretched on, and after two months with no green light in sight, real estate agents I hadn't seen in years were suddenly seeking out my company. Financial insecurity must have been leaking from my pores. There are pheromones that the body secretes when faced with danger, lactating pheromones, sexual attraction pheromones, and I suspect there are real estate commission pheromones that signal your home may be in play.

"You must let me sell your house," said Fiona, who, like many real estate agents, got her start after her divorce by monetizing her Rolodex, her impeccable taste, and her friends' divorces. I agreed to let her try because there's something about her perfectly symmetrical bone structure and the way she accessorizes that hypnotizes people into carrying out her wishes. Also, she promised to fleece someone for an absurdly bloated amount of money. After a brisk walk-through, she called to inform me that the house had boatloads of what brokers euphemistically refer to as "deferred maintenance," which is code for "your home is one step up from a cave dwelling," and I never heard from Fiona again.

Then I ran into Dina, the seller's agent who represented the Widow McGarry, in the produce section of a local organic food market.

As I shook a cantaloupe, Dina offered a kind of "I've been there, sister" sympathy, suggesting that we go on a hike, do shots, and get Brazilians together. OK, she didn't suggest waxing, but she assured me that not only could she sell my house, she had the perfect place for me to relocate.

"Everyone in our neighborhood moves into the Manor when they get divorced," she explained. The Manor is a well-maintained glass high-rise, about ten blocks from my home. I pictured a kind of divorce underground railroad, with Dina ushering the recently unwed from their houses into the Manor.

"I was married and living a few blocks from you. After my divorce, I moved in. That's how I got into the real estate business. I'm the exclusive agent for the condominium association."

By the time we reached the ancient grains, she'd talked me into an open house that was coincidentally happening *right now*. As we exited the store, she waved to the cashier. Did Dina have some sort of arrangement with the management? She hadn't made any purchases.

The Manor was two blocks away. Groceries in tow, I agreed that the galley kitchen seemed only the tiniest bit plasticky after twenty-one years in a home that's nearly one hundred years old, the plumbing soundlessly efficient, and that the view of the city was expansive. There was something seductive about the idea of living somewhere where all the corners meet and effluence is silently and swiftly whisked away.

When she opened a shallow broom closet, I gasped, wondering how I would break it to Ezra that this cubicle was their bedroom post graduation. As we peeked into the Lilliputian bathroom, Dina casually mentioned that the day before I'd closed escrow on my house, she'd opened a built-in cabinet in the master bedroom closet and discovered stacks of hundred-dollar bills. They totaled one hundred, maybe two hundred thousand dollars.

"I returned it, of course. You know, the McGarrys were extraordinarily wealthy. Yours was one of several homes they owned, including a house on the beach near the Hearst castle in San Simeon."

This was news to me. If only the McGarrys had repaired the sinking foundation and put in copper pipes. If I'd found that stash, I'd have been able to make those improvements and sell the house for a Fiona-sized sum. But they didn't and I didn't. I thanked Dina, headed home to refrigerate my melon, and by the time I arrived, Dina had emailed the price of the condo and what she thought she could get for the house. I gave the house a quick once-over, checking for loose floorboards or a hidden safe. The Divorcée Dormitory would have to wait. I emailed Grace.

"Hey there, Grace! We're thinking that a kitchen remodel will be too much of a pain in the neck!! You know how those things always take longer than you think. LOL!!! Also, we'd like to try and qualify for one of those solar rebates while the government is still offering them so, just wondering if we halve the amount we applied for, would that speed up getting our loan approved?"

I wept in Grace's cubicle as we initialed each page of our new mortgage documents.

"I'm just so happy that we'll finally be able to update the bathroom or upgrade to solar. Solar is so important."

In full view of Grace, we headed off in opposite directions. Grace Lee, loan officer and unwitting patron saint of financially strapped un-trothing, had the courtesy or compassion, I'll never know which, not to call us out. Then again, perhaps it was our undercurrent of contempt that made her assume us to be your average long-marrieds.

Holding on to the home turned out to be a good decision, because shortly after that, I discovered that in midlife, deep closets are almost as essential an asset as deep pockets.

Stuffed

WEDDING PHOTOS HAD MIGRATED INTO Band-Aid boxes, a charm bracelet belonging to my mother had coupled with a pair of ear buds and were inexorably conjoined in a desk drawer, and what was a baseball-shaped birthday candle doing inside a bag of sweet potato fries in the deep recesses of the freezer? When you occupy the same house for more than twenty years, stuff settles into the nooks and crannies like fossilized evidence of family life. On a scale of homey to Grey Gardens, my house was closer to homey, but behind closed doors, there was clutter enough to fill another two houses. Why organize albums when you can pack thousands of photos into every piece of furniture you own? That's what drawers are for. Remaining in the marriage long after legions of counselors threw up their hands in exasperation allowed me to put off cleaning out our closets.

Every so often I'd do a purge, but soon enough, other items rushed in to fill the gaps. My home seemed proof of the steady-state cosmology theory. This theory tells us that the universe is always expanding but maintains a constant average density, with matter being continuously created to form new stars and galaxies at the same rate that old ones become unobservable, so it always appears to have the same density. The steady-state theory was debunked and supplanted with the big bang theory in the 1960s (my Florida science textbooks never reflected that update), and it may not be true of the universe at large, but a case could be made that in the cosmology of family dwellings, it is fully operational.

My days were punctuated with pleasant reminders of my role in the family, the community, and the world at large. In her book *The Object Parade*, essayist Dinah Lenney observes the role that objects play in our lives: "Things ordinary and extraordinary tether us to place and people and the past, to feeling and thought, to each other and ourselves."

I have stuff, therefore I am.

The nest had emptied of humans (if momentarily), but I wound up with everybody's crap. There was the typical stuff that children leave behind: trophies, papier-mâché piggy banks, enough baseball uniforms to outfit several teams. Then there were the frustratingly dismembered toys that might otherwise have been donated or sold: a hand-carved wooden Amish (antique?) model plane missing a wing; vintage (maybe collectors' items?) Barbie and Ken dolls with their heads lopped off, replaced with penguin and sea lion finger puppets; an RMS *Titanic* puzzle with pieces missing from the hull (irony unintended?).

In Ezra's hasty college packing spree, the entire ecosystem of the house had been disturbed, like how a tsunami washes over and then deposits debris in its wake. What had been out of view now covered every surface. High school essays I saved; math quizzes I chucked. Reams of SAT and ACT practice materials received the ol' heave-ho. Kid artwork presented a greater challenge. As if punishment for being the kind of parent who'd lavished culturally enriching opportunities upon my offspring, I was drowning in doodles, sketch pads, and DIY manga. The walls were already decorated with favored pieces. Ezra was talented, but no Picasso. Even Picasso's mother might have had the same thought when culling the most precious of his childhood drawings: "Pablo's talented, but he's no El Greco."

Socks trailed from the laundry room to the bedroom, where pants, underwear, and T-shirts lay rumpled on the floor. It was less like Ezra left for college and more like they'd been raptured.

Waterford crystal bowls took up an entire shelf above the fridge. Unsurprisingly, my ex hadn't taken any with him when he moved out. A fresh start would feel weighted down by wedding crystal. But what was I supposed to do with these leaden reminders of our nuptials? Some enterprising person should offer BYOW Divorce Nights at smash rooms, also known as rage rooms. If I were invited to a party where I could bring my Waterford bowls and be issued a baseball bat to smash them, that's an invitation I'd accept.

When my ex departed, it appeared that he'd only packed an overnight bag for a weekend getaway. He left behind a walk-in closet packed floor to ceiling with twenty years' worth of scripts he'd written, every one of our expensively framed wedding pictures, his grandmother's dining room furniture, and a two-feet-by-two-feet framed oil painting that Bob, my father-in-law, sent as a wedding present. It's a portrait of Bob that is inscribed BEST DAD IN THE WHOLE WORLD. What was I supposed to do with that? My ex had something of a sunglasses fetish; cabinets were crammed with empty cases. Like a snake shedding his skin, he'd slithered on, but these empty husks remained.

Also, a cache of nude pictures I'd begrudgingly posed for after much cajoling. I don't understand the desire to photograph anything served up at a restaurant or in flagrante delicto. I've never snapped a shot of even the most artfully plated charcuterie nor asked anyone to send a picture of their genitals—if anything, I find it a turn-on to receive a picture of someone wearing as many items of clothing as possible, short of a cape.

Feeling silly and self-conscious, I'd assumed suggestive postures while performing otherwise ordinary household activities. Legs splayed on a divan, I am brushing my teeth. Bent over for a backdoor view, I am removing the ring around the bathtub. One leg astride the bed, I'm reconciling the gas bill, *tout nu*. It's an acquired taste for sure, "chore" porn, but my ex had held on to them for the entirety of our marriage, so leaving them behind felt like a sucker punch. I would have preferred they were shredded, burned at an altar to my enduring beauty, or at minimum disposed of discreetly, double-bagged in our recycling bin.

In the nightstand next to our bed, I discovered an X-rated love letter I'd written ten years prior, nail clippings, and dust. I'd read once that 80 percent of household dust is skin; this turns out to be not true, but I felt a responsibility to return this mystery matter; after all, it was in the nightstand on his side of the bed. I shoveled the contents of the drawer into an envelope and mailed it to his new address. I don't know if it ever arrived because he was gracious enough to never mention it. This was not my finest moment.

My new solitary existence amid so much ephemera might have

been manageable, except that in between my kid's and husband's exits, both of my parents died. My sister and I were tasked with dispensing with their belongings.

Of the many markers that define both Gen X and baby boomers, we're the last for whom trolling exes required more than armchair detective work, we're the last whose late-night screens showed an American flag waving in the breeze accompanied by the national anthem, and we may be the last that are saddled with physical memorabilia. Our children are citizens of the cloud, so we're practically an endangered species. You could call us Generation Stuff. This becomes especially true after your parents die.

It was all so sudden. Both of them, in their late seventies, had underlying issues that had seemed to be kept at bay. We hadn't noticed our father's slowing down, and when he had a stroke and was unable to recover from heart surgery, we assumed our mother would have years ahead of her. Maybe even a racy final chapter. At the senior home, a klatch of ambulatory gentlemen lined up to sit at her table in the dining room every night. But a month after his death, her health deteriorated, and then just hours before our father's memorial service was to start, she died. Family who'd flown in to mourn our father arrived only to be informed that our mother had passed too. Guests swooned with grief. It was like a scene in a black comedy.

I'm sure that Lisa and I were in some altered state. When my sister, whose efficiency is bested only by robots, decided that we should quickly close out our parents' two-bedroom unit to save on paying the next month's rent. We set to work right after the memorial service and reception.

The plan was to create two distinct piles. One containing items to be picked up by a local thrift store, and another for movers to pack up and ship to my sister in New York and me in Los Angeles.

We worked for two days straight. Alternating between bouts of grief and bursts of energy, it might be the closest I have come to a hallucinogenic experience. Some of our choices, in retrospect, are head-scratchers. Did we keep my father's collection of professional-grade cooking knives? Nope. Instead, I carefully preserved three packages of plastic chip clips like reliquary. My sister insisted that we each take one of my mother's rusting colanders, circa 1970-something. I flatly refused but she doesn't take no for an answer, which is why, when searching for my ID at airport security, I discovered that she'd snuck the smaller one into my carry-on tote.

You learn a lot about people by what they leave behind. If it were to come to light that my mother had been a CIA operative, I wouldn't be surprised. I knew she had meticulously assembled family photo albums, including photographs of relatives that no one, including her, recognized, but she also kept extensive paperwork. In her expandable accordion files were smaller files, and in each section of those files were even smaller folders, like a Russian doll of nonessential data. Her date books (also in the folders) listed the birthdays of every living cousin, even ones she was no longer on speaking terms with, which were numerous.

One thing you can't imagine when you're a child is that the letters and birthday cards you send to your parents will one day be returned to you. These now served as proof of what an outstanding daughter my older sister was and how I was the worst child in recorded history. Maybe not Lizzie Borden territory, but Lisa's file included a handmade "coupon" book labeled "To Mom and Dad:

gifts of service and thoughtfulness." Inside are offerings: "This coupon is redeemable anytime for dishwashing/vacuuming/ironing." In my file: an unsigned postcard that reads "This camp makes you write home if you want dinner on Friday night" and another reading simply "Send me money, candy, and gum!" I put these aside to be sent to my home before my sister could see them to avert future blackmail opportunities, and also as a reminder to start my own filing system.

There were some items I was sure I wanted to hold on to, like a set of dishes that belonged to my grandmother, and I couldn't imagine parting with my mother's needlepointed pillows, even though I couldn't imagine living with them either. Ditto for assorted items of clothing, art, and some large pieces of furniture. Because I had the larger storage capacity, we decided to send memorabilia we couldn't make a decision on to my home, confident that the family heirlooms had value—if not sentimental, then monetary.

My mother had great taste. Even when we lived in a shoebox-sized apartment with an avocado-colored kitchenette and industrial-grade carpets, she'd furnished it with elegant antiques culled from estate sales and country auctions. Armed with scholarly guides to Chinese dynastical markings, she'd amassed an extensive collection of Chinese altar fruit, cloisonné,* and an array of textiles. She'd also pawed through thrift-store dollar boxes, so what was what? Of all the information she might have kept that would have been useful, she'd neglected to record her possessions' provenance.

---

* This is an elaborate enamel technique in which copper threading is woven through decorative enamel designs.

When my parents' finances crumbled, my mother brought two Cycladic fertility statuettes to Sotheby's to be appraised. She was informed they had no measurable value. In an uncharacteristic fit of anger, she'd thrown one of them against a garage wall. A few weeks later, Sotheby's called to say that they'd made a mistake and that one of the figures might bring $10,000 at auction. It was the one she'd damaged, which of course was now worthless. Surely there were other items she hadn't been able to part with that might be as valuable?

By the time the moving van pulled up, I was the sole inhabitant of the house. Now I had my stuff, my ex's stuff, my kid's stuff, and my parents' stuff, as well as the stuff they inherited from their parents.

The delivery from Florida included the sarcophagi. They're not actual coffins, but the two matching sturdy mahogany clothing armoires, four by ten feet, that my parents had owned for as long as I could remember, did look a tad funereal. I'd paid $2,000 to have them sent across the country, in addition to the other moving fees, and when they arrived, they appeared to be more ornately carved, immaculately cared for, and, distressingly, more massive than I'd remembered. I wasn't sure how or where they'd fit in my house, so I looked up prices and sales outlets for ornately carved, immaculately cared for, massive mahogany armoires and learned that every single ornately carved, immaculately cared for, massive mahogany armoire ever made was now on sale.

It was then I happened onto a 2017 *Forbes* article titled "Sorry, No One Wants Your Parents' Stuff," in which writer Richard Eisenberg chronicles the frustrations of securing new homes for the items he'd inherited from his parents. "Heirloom today, gone tomorrow" is how he characterizes the fate of what he called "browns," heavy wooden dark furniture, like the armoires.

"Unless your parents collected eighteenth-century French antiques, there isn't a market for the kinds of furniture and objects our parents collected." That's what Joanna, the representative from Everything But the House, a newish online estate sale outfit that Eisenberg endorsed in his essay, wrote to me after I'd emailed photos of the armoires. She gently suggested I'd be better off donating everything I'd had sent and taking the tax write-off, but I wasn't ready to relegate "Mom and Dad," as I'd started addressing them, to a dusty corner at Goodwill.

The only room they (barely) fit in was the master bedroom. Side by side, they loomed over the bed. I delighted in demonstrating to friends how I could stand comfortably inside, pounding on the door, calling out to be released, just for shits and giggles. This might be one of the reasons friends worried if I'd ever date again.

UNPACKING THE OTHER BOXES, I found items I remembered having sent—like my grandmother's dishes, which I immediately sent off to Ezra—and the assortment of Chinese porcelain objects. Like pennies in a drawer, they seemed to have multiplied on the trip west. I placed a grouping of passion fruit, pomegranate, and a few melons in a tight clump on the fireplace mantel, hoping that might minimize the tchotchke effect, even though they might be from an important dynasty.

But I had zero memory of arranging transport for a numbered

print depicting two Botero-esque female figures.* They seem to be siblings, standing in close familial proximity, arranging flowers in a vase. I hung it in my foyer. An entire year passed before I noticed a detail I'd missed during my entire childhood. The women have no faces. Have I entertained the idea that facial features were once there and have now morphed into blank ovals? Have I worried that if I try to get rid of the painting it will somehow find its way back to me, no matter what hidey-hole I leave it in? Yep. It's in my garage now, facing the wall, and I won't be surprised if the next time I check in on it the figures have shifted positions.

Of all the assorted odds and ends, there was one thing I was certain held only sentimental value: my father's Rolex. At some flush point in time, he'd owned an authentic Rolex. This watch had heft, but on closer inspection, it was an authentic Rolax. There's an A where the E should be. I like to imagine that my Rolax might be that one factory mistake making it worth millions, and I'll get my *Antiques Roadshow* knocked-off-my-feet moment,† but even I know that the chances are greater that the creepy painting is haunted. The watch doesn't run, but it does make me laugh.

As my parents' stuff migrated into my house, each unexpected encounter now seemed a ghastly reminder of how much my role as mother, wife, and dutiful (if, initially, begrudging) daughter had changed. Reaching into my makeup bag for my Burt's Bees lip

---

* During the 1970s, every suburban family acquired at least one creepy piece of fine-ish art that was displayed in a prominent place to demonstrate their appreciation of art.

† In 2020, a guest at an *Antiques Roadshow* appraisal in South Dakota fell backward in shock upon learning that a Rolex purchased in 1974 for $345 was a collector's item worth between 500 and 700 thousand.

balm might result in my pulling out my mother's lipstick, her sole indulgence, Chanel's Fatale. While perusing Pema Chodron's *When Things Fall Apart*, a flyer for No Exit, my ex's Sartre-inspired high school band, might sail out from between the pages.

Paring down the surfeit of souvenirs required a detachment that I couldn't muster. I was unpacking and then repacking items, but I couldn't fit things back into the boxes they'd arrived in, so I loaded up laundry baskets and moved excess kid crap, ex leftovers, and parental memorabilia into the garage. Only I ran out of baskets, so I wound up dumping things onto the floor.

Once a teenage hangout room, it was now close to a Superfund site. As it is also home to emergency canned tuna, calcified energy bars, and decades-old bottled water, it's possible that something is growing in there besides the shame that keeps me from dealing with it. When one of my dearest friends noted that she'd never been in my garage, I replied, "Because then I'd have to kill you."

THREE YEARS HAVE PASSED. I haven't yet been able to hold objects close and ask "Does it spark joy?" as Marie Kondo instructed. Kondo was in her late twenties when that book was published. As someone in my late fifties, I have a tough time accepting that joy is the best metric. There are quite a few things I value deeply, that I've held close, including my kid, and joy is not the feeling evoked.

Each time I pull into my driveway, I'm astonished at my good fortune to have taken the Widow McGarry's place. *Hello, old friend*, I think upon entering, and then I practice saying goodbye. The day will come, sometime between tomorrow and the next few years, when I will move into a space that's half the size of my house, if that.

Best-case scenario, the Divorcée Dormitory. How many pounds of stuff will I need to lose to fit into one of those 850-square-foot condos? Dina will guide my passage with a flashlight as I lug the entirety of my belongings in a plastic garbage bag.

Until then, the garage remains stuffed, its contents layered like those pie charts of the earth's sediment beds depicted in children's science books. Stacks of bongs, sheets of school photos we ordered too many of, my dad's collection of casino windbreakers.

What will I take with me? Surely I can find room for my mother's insect pin? Everyone's mother had one. Cartier's gold and ruby ladybugs were hugely popular. Joan Rivers had a vast collection that included a crystal-encrusted grasshopper. My mother's was an ordinary housefly.

I will find a place for a birthday gift from Ezra that I've been saving in my files. "Dear Mom, I know that my gift giving is counterintuitive because it's your money, but I said, 'Hey, why not!' Love, Ez." It's written on a five-dollar In-N-Out Burger gift card.

There is also my most cherished object, liberated from my father's desk, which I intend to take with me wherever I wind up, along with the Rolax. It's a stop-sign-red Staples Easy Button.

I hold it close and it whispers sweet nothings.

"That was easy."

"Your house, your rules."

"Because you said so."

"Of course you're right."

It really does produce something close to joy.

Silver Nesting

LANDLADY. BANISH THE IMAGE OF a world-weary Depression-era crone, cigarette dangling from her lips, blousy house-dress and slippers. These days, it's world-weary, yoga-panted, almond-latte-drinking, Dansko clog–clad crones like me, clearing space for a stranger's toothbrush on the bathroom vanity.

Articles about us typically feature women extolling the virtues of house sharing. In 2017, *The New York Times* ran a story about a San Francisco woman who began renting out four of the five bedrooms in her home after her kids left for college and her husband died. Pictured in California casual, pastel sweater and white jeans, she's cheerfully greeting a family from Belgium who will stay with her for a week. "I'm really enjoying meeting new people and being able to pay my mortgage," she enthuses. I hit the arrow on the slideshow over and over, like a monkey, trying to find the shots of her hoisting loads of laundry, scrubbing toilet bowls, and spot treating the grease stain on her couch where her boarders ate chips while enjoying the pricey cable package she must provide to keep them happy. What kind of gloves does she wear when disposing of the odd used condom? What face when she discovers a web of hairs of unknown origin clogging the shower drain? Odd, how the *Times* neglected to include those images.

I'd never had great luck with roommates. College roommate number one contracted elephantiasis during the first week of school and was removed from our dorm room on a stretcher. I never saw her again. The second dropped out to join Up with People, the cultish, relentlessly optimistic traveling youth performing group. I never saw her again either. My last roommate and I were a terrible match. She had a cocaine habit and blasted Bowie's "Young Americans" from her corner of our prison cell–sized quarters, which didn't mesh well with my pot smoking and endless looping of the saddest of James Taylor's sad songs. I never saw her again either, but she has become something of a cult figure in the hardcore punk music scene. She is known for her "rage and pain-filled vocals" as the front woman of Lower East Side doomsday prophets I.C.U.*

In my twenties and thirties, I lived alone for long stretches and couldn't imagine cohabitating worth the inconvenience and lack of privacy, but back then I had the inflated self-importance of youth to keep me company. After nineteen years of parenting and twenty-one cohabitating, I'd grown accustomed to the reliable hubbub produced by a child and even a marriage in decline. But I'm a few DNA strands short of human before my morning coffee. I am given

---

* That is the description of her vocal stylings at allmusic.com. I've never seen them perform live, but I can attest that after viewing several videos, the vocals are, indeed, rage and pain-filled.

to tuneless humming, and cereal boxes I've opened look like raccoons have ransacked the kitchen cabinets. I'm the first to admit I'm not for everyone. I'm more of an acquired taste. So, roomies? At this age?

It wasn't until I handed over the entire refinancing check to my ex that the enormity of single-handedly running the household sank in. Mortgage. Insurance. Property taxes. Roof maintenance. Tree maintenance. Plumbing maintenance. HVAC maintenance. I didn't have a clue what HVAC stood for and I still don't, but I hope, whatever it is, it's . . . maintaining.

My friend Patty suggested I game the system. A gig-economy ninja, she's a writer, actress, and teacher, but her most lucrative side hustle is renting out her home.

"You'll make more money if you lease out your entire place for short-term rentals. I'm starting a business to help people get rental ready. I can show you the ropes."

"Sounds great! And where will I be living? In my car?"

She explained her strategy. She rents her home at a premium rate, packs up her two terriers and twin daughters, moves into less expensive digs, and pockets the difference. "Sometimes it goes wonky," she warned. Recently, a family showed up three hours early and, because of a language barrier, didn't understand when she said, "I need time to get the place ready, why don't you go out for lunch?" Instead, they planted themselves in her cozy den and looked on in bewilderment as she raced around picking up laundry, washing down surfaces, and patching a section of tiling that had picked an inconvenient time to tear away from a bathroom wall. While wishing them a nice stay, she leaned against a curtain and the entire window treatment collapsed. In her haste, on the drive to her rental, she ran out of gas, and her carload of refrigerated foods spoiled in the blazing Los Angeles heat. Two days into their stay, the family asked for their money back, and she had to eat the nonrefundable rental fee on her cheaper place. She shrugged as she relayed the story. Patty chops her own wood and is handy with a caulking gun. She demoed a wall in her kitchen. I needed an Advil just hearing about her ordeal. My version of the story would end with the words "And that's how I ended up addicted to OxyContin."

I decided to go the route that provided more stability, like my friend Christine, who's been renting out rooms in her home since her divorce almost a decade ago. "Outside of one tenant who had a psychotic break and had to be institutionalized, it's been amazing. And everyone is doing it. Everyone."

Or my friend Jan, a teacher and a divorcée who held onto the large family home after her three kids left for college. It's a good thing she stayed in the house because all three have returned for varying lengths of time; one came home for a gap year that lasted for three. Her goddaughter has been renting a bedroom since the kids went off to school. In their midtwenties now, only one of her offspring is self-supporting, so the extra cash has been welcome.

"My goddaughter is the perfect boarder. She goes to school full time, has a boyfriend who lives across town, and she sleeps at his place a lot. Also, she might be anorexic, because she never eats at home."

A busy person with an eating disorder who sleeps around: that sounded ideal!

The explosion in midlife folks, primarily women, renting out spare bedrooms in their house has led to any number of roommate matching services like Nesterly and Roommates4Boomers. We, who once debated being Rachels, Monicas, or Phoebes, are now vying for who gets to be Blanche or Dorothy from *The Golden Girls*. Silver Nesting Roommates is such a service. For a one-time fee of fifty dollars, homeowners are matched with a tenant. The charge includes a cursory amount of vetting, including background, credit, and criminal record checks. Still, if you're a catfishing predator looking to fleece older women, Silver Nesting takes the work out of finding a mark.*

If every picture tells a story, then each picture of the houses available for sharing at Silver Nesting tells you that you're looking at the home of a middle-aged woman.

One host treats us to a shot of magazines on a coffee table. A magnifying glass rests on top of her copy of *Reader's Digest Large Print*. Next to that, a hand-held paper fan, the kind old-fashioned churches hand out in the South, which menopausal women whip out when surprised by a hot flash in a location where ripping their clothes off might be unwelcome.

One set of photographs worried me enough that I wondered if I should call social services. The homeowner noted that she was a collector, so there was "a lot to look at" in her home. Surfaces that weren't occupied by stacks of clothing were populated with Hummel figurines. An unmade bed, pillows deeply creased—indicative of someone spending an awful lot of time reclining—had a digital alarm clock, circa 1973, on an adjacent bedside table. There was a full-sized harp in the living room. I want to believe we live in a

---

* House sharing that pairs intergenerational roommates is another growing market. The nonprofit New York Foundation for Senior Citizens pair seniors who need help to afford their rent or mortgage and household chores with young would-be renters. Big surprise, most of the seniors are female.

world where someone looks past the hoardery aspects and thinks, *what luck, she's got a harp and I play the harp! I'll take it!*

Under a section labeled "What I'm Looking For," Hoardery Harpist wrote, "I don't know." The website offers ample opportunity to review your answers. Ostensibly, she'd reviewed this assessment and concluded, *yeah, the idea that I am looking for a roommate is so far from anything I'd imagined myself doing*, so that "I don't know" summed it up just fine, and she hit submit.

What was I looking for in a tenant? I didn't know either, but I was racked with anxiety. The prospect of inviting someone into my home seemed even more fraught than entering the dating world. Hooking up might not involve as much intimacy as bumping into someone before my first espresso.

It wasn't until I started floating the idea that I remembered that my dear friend, character actor Taylor Negron, had once resided at the Writers' Villa, just up the street from me. The Villa was owned by Cathi Davis, a real estate agent who hosted writers, actors, and comedians including Taylor, Ellen DeGeneres, and Paula Poundstone in her Mediterranean-style Spanish mansion. George Clooney's ex-wife, actress Talia Balsam, lived there. She and George threw parties in the courtyard. For twenty years, Cathi catered lavish spreads and provided emotional support for her beloved tenants. My daily run took me past her home, but I'd been unaware of her or her gracious villa until September 26, 2012, when one of her tenants, a bit player on the series *Sons of Anarchy*, went crazy on bath salts. He killed Cathi, strangled her cat, slashed her art collection, and then, believing he had the power of flight, launched himself from a second-story balcony. He didn't survive the crash landing onto the driveway. I never had the good fortune to meet Cathi, described by Taylor as "a near saint" in a tribute published by *xoJane*.

Maybe, like in the Villa's heydays, my home could be a refuge for a cadre of lively artists. But with Cathi's final tenant in mind, I decided to rent only to someone within my circle of acquaintances.

I dashed off an email to everyone I could think of who might know someone who might know someone who might want to be my roomie. After two weeks, I had three possible candidates. With great trepidation as to whom I had reeled in, I set up the first interview.

Remember when you sent away for sea monkeys as a kid? The colorful ads in the back pages of comic books depicted a smiling, waving sea monkey family. The father, tall and lean, held a pipe in his hand, or rather, his tentacled paw. The mother sea monkey sported a buoyant blond bob topped with a golden crown. The child had his own crown and was leaning on a baseball bat, or maybe I just imagined that. But when the package arrived at your house, you'd pour the silty powder into the bowl that formerly housed your goldfish, and soon it was teeming with slimy, stinky brine shrimp. If you listened very closely, on any given day in suburban America in the 1970s, you could hear the sound of children crying as brine shrimp were flushed into watery oblivion.

What would arrive at my doorstep? Sea monkey or brine shrimp?

Red Flags

THERE ARE FEW UNIVERSALLY RECOGNIZED symbols, but most people around the globe can agree that when someone gives you the middle finger, it means "fuck off." A thumbs-up indicates that the coast is clear, and a red flag is a sign of a problem that needs attention. Sometimes in life, red flags are waving right in front of us. We simply choose to ignore them.

A flag with three vertical stripes of blue, white, and red has another meaning altogether. That's the flag of France, and I'm a sucker for all things French, which is why I was elated when I answered the door to my first candidate, the son of a friend's friend from summer camp. We'd had only one brief email exchange, which he signed with the initial J. I'd had no clue that he was Parisian.

Jean Luc was twenty-seven, tall, slim, big sad French eyes, motorbike helmet in his hand. He said "Bonjour." It was all I could do to stop myself from saying, "Welcome to your new home, roomie."

As an undergraduate at NYU, I came down with a raging case

of Francophilia during Intro to New Wave Cinema. After a youth
spent basking in the unrelenting sunshine and kitschiness of Miami
Beach, the moody, languid films of Truffaut, Varda, and Goddard
were a welcome tonic. The school also afforded me the chance to in-
teract with foreign students. A classmate joked that the first stop for
male exchange students after landing at JFK was my dorm room.
There was the distant musician from Auvergne, the withholding
director from Lorraine, the elusive architect from Languedoc—but
he might have been gay, so it was understandable that he was always
running off to other assignations. How could I forget the remote Al-
satian, who was majoring in ennui with a minor in melancholy? I
loved the lilting, vainglorious way they pronounced my name, *Anna-
bella*, while informing me that although we were dating, they'd still
be seeing other people. It had been decades since my last French
connection, but my soft spot for the French has never waned.

Jean Luc immediately launched into his predicament. I could
only make out every other word. "Recently graduated from NYU ...
cross-country road trip with friend ... falling-out with friend ... terrible situation ... no longer speaking ... all of my belongings ... a
storage unit." Was it that he'd had a falling-out with his friend that
he'd gone across the country with, or was it a disagreement with
the one with whom he'd been renting a place? Were his belongings
in storage, or was he living in a storage unit? I couldn't divine the
exact circumstances, but the message was clear: "Bad things have
happened since I arrived in Los Angeles."

I was such a nervous wreck that I could only hear my heart
pounding in my eardrums. Choices make me anxious. Cereal
aisles with their floor-to-ceiling offerings overwhelm me. I can't be
trusted in big-box stores. I'll go in to buy strawberries and walk

out with lawn furniture. It's one of the reasons I decided against online dating. All that teeth and hair—or, in my age range, receding hairlines. How can one possibly choose? Though I needed the extra income, I hadn't yet figured out criteria by which to evaluate potential boarders.

As he relayed his tale of woe, I was reminded of how everyone's story about moving to Los Angeles sounds similar. The newly transplanted are invariably stunned by the vastness of the sprawl, the sameness of the mini-malls, and the traffic that drains your will to live. I was tempted to say as much, but I didn't, because he'd said "Hello" in French.

My hearing kicked back in as he explained he was working as a receptionist at a Pilates studio in Santa Monica. More bad news for him, as Santa Monica is at least an hour's drive from my home, but good news for me. The commute would add to the hours he'd be out of the house. I explained that the kitchen, dining room, and living room would be common spaces and held my breath, hoping he would like *la chambre*. His eyes lit up when I showed him the guest quarters.

"This is amazing. Living here would be the best to have happened to me since I moved to Los Angeles."

Jean Luc had so much going for him as a tenant. He was the one and only candidate I'd met. He was French, didn't seem at all murdery, and he was offering me money. But almost as enticing was the chance to be a part of changing someone's luck. Jean Luc offered a chance to restore my sense of usefulness. Then, the kicker.

"Would it be OK if friends from Paris came to visit?"

Would it be OK? I imagined Parisians lounging in my living room, debating the merits of Claire Denis versus Marie NDiaye.

I'd been worried about the monasterial silence of an empty nest, but just like Cathi, I'd be running my own artist colony! I couldn't resist.

As is typical, when faced with a truly important decision, I approached it with all the planning of someone fleeing a burning house. I've made several major life decisions in this way—moves across the country, marriages—reasoning that if I think too hard about it, I'll never do it.

Jean Luc was set to join my household in a few weeks, but two days after the interview, he stopped by in a panic.

"Did you hear about the accident?"

"No, where would I have heard about it?"

Only someone in their twenties thinks people keep abreast of every detail of their lives. He'd had an accident . . . his motorbike was totaled . . . he was getting screwed by the driver of the car he'd collided with. The upshot was that more bad things had happened and he was going to need to move in earlier than expected. It should have been a red flag, but I was focused on my good fortune.

The night prior to Jean Luc's arrival, I reviewed my life choices, seemingly encapsulated in the unexpected trajectory of one hundred square feet. The bedroom had been *un petit* playroom, then a guest room where my parents had stayed, then my spouse's office. Finally, it had become known as the "punishment room" because my spouse and I had been relegated to sleep there after arguments. Unable to afford two places, my ex had spent the last year of our marriage in solitary in the punishment room.

I'd been working out of town when my ex moved out, and as I readied the bedroom, I discovered dust bunnies the size of koala bears under the bed. It occurred to me, only then, that he'd been disengaged from our marriage for longer than I'd realized. People often note when one partner emotionally exits the relationship, but a better indicator of the health of a relationship might be tracking participation in household chores. He'd always been fastidious. The dust bunnies were a red flag I'd failed to register.

Two of Jean Luc's gregarious friends showed up to help him move in. A good sign. Then, as they were leaving, one of his pals turned to me and said, "Just keep him alive."

Danger, Will Robinson, danger!

That evening, I let Jean Luc know that a few close friends were stopping by for an intimate re-housewarming party, my first gathering since the ex moved out. I hadn't said *not* to come, nor had I invited him. As I looked over at him, drink in hand, chatting up my friends and neighbors, it would be the first but not the last time during his tenure that reminded me of an episode in the actor Charles Grodin's memoir. Grodin was shooting a film in a castle in England, and when he attempted to chat up the lord of the manor, the gentleman retorted, "It would be so nice if you weren't here."

IN THE BEGINNING WAS THE word, and the word was . . . bacon. The sound of bacon sizzling accompanied his cranking up my espresso machine each morning at 5:00 a.m. The scent wafted up the stairwell into my bedroom, invading my sleep. It seeped into everything, like black mold or a lingering depression. You might think you've gotten it under control, but nope, every day you wake up and *it's still there.*

Just when I'd successfully flushed the heavy odor of the

morning's rasher from the house, he'd arrive back home and begin preparing supper. The smell was so strong, I half expected to see that he'd dug a pit into the living room floor and was roasting a pig. It wasn't just bacon for breakfast, it was all bacon, all the time.

A grease stain, caramel in color, began forming on the kitchen ceiling. Oblong shaped, like the Ile Saint-Louis. My refrigerator resembled a meat locker. He stocked it with bacon strips, bacon bits for seasoning, and jars of bacon fat. It's possible he was also using the drippings as pomade because I often caught a whiff of pork when he walked by.

On film sets, the French have a practice of rolling meals. The caterers crank out meals continually so you can eat while working. It's called "French hours," and that's what my house was like. Any time Jean Luc was in the house, he was preparing a multi-course feast.

More exasperating than the realization that my closet smelled like a smokehouse was that I'd lost my appetite. Since my kid left for college, food had lost its pleasure. Eating seemed like a tiresome chore. Get up, eat, work, eat more, why? I'd heard others describe this kind of thing. A friend in Sarasota, Florida, told me that after she divorced and her kids left home, she'd opened her fridge one morning and was startled to discover only vodka and gelato. *That'll never happen to me.*

My cupboards were bare, my refrigerator empty. Staring into the stark whiteness was almost blinding—like looking directly into the sun. I made one or two attempts at convivial cooking for one but gave it up because I felt like a minor player in a Wes Anderson film. I pictured a long tracking shot, the exterior walls of our homes removed, the camera panning past one dwelling after another where legions of us, recently empty-nested, doll-like female figures, sat alone at our dinner tables.

Meals consisted of shoving something in my mouth while standing over the sink: a hunk of rice cheese, with all the flavor of a glue stick, placed on top of a rice cake, about as appetizing as particle board seasoned with dust. Dinner might find me gnawing on a heel of bread, scarfing down a container of blackberries, or chewing through a stalk of celery. Not that it was at all slimming. Another meal might be an entire bag of lentil chips, which, it turns out, have more than twice the calories of Lays. *Just eat the damn potato chips!* I was consuming only one food at a time; even combining ingredients seemed pointlessly taxing. I didn't feel I merited the effort. Watching Jean Luc take pleasure in carefully seasoning his meats, assembling colorful arrays of vegetables, made me feel sadder by comparison. Even if I wanted to prepare food, I couldn't, because the resident chef took up so much space.

When not foraging for my pitiful fare, I was scrambling for work and feeling the weight of running the household. In no short order, the plumbing backed up. The water heater expired. "A branch of your maple tree is hanging over my garage and needs to be trimmed," my neighbor informed me. Still reeling from the deaths of my parents, mourning the loss of the marriage, pining for my child, the missing cat, the carpool, and my tennis class, I took to skulking around my house to try to avoid Jean Luc. It was impossible. He wasn't just living in my home—it was more like an occupation.

Toward the end of November, the holidays in full swing, a care package from his parents arrived. It was a selection of delicacies from D'artagnan, a French specialty shop in New York. It contained all manner of duck products. Duck innards, duck sausage, pâté, foie gras, and duck butter. My ex had a thing for duck. I've never liked gamey meats—even the smell turns my stomach—and now it was a sorrowful, high-saturated-fat reminder of my marriage. Each morning, I'd peek into the refrigerator and try to estimate how many days until he'd make his way through the duck. Just when the stash dwindled down to one tub of duck butter, D'artagnan mistakenly sent a second package, identical to the first. Its arrival was greeted as though it were the second coming, which, technically, it was.

When not manning the stove, Jean Luc would settle into the backyard couch with a glass of wine or five and binge-watch TV shows on his computer. Smoking one cigarette after another, he would stop only to alternate with smoking weed until bedtime. If there were high northerly winds, my house smelled like a weed dispensary. If the wind was blowing away from the house, it smelled like an average college dorm room, if that room was located inside a French brasserie.

The United States officially declared war on drugs in 1971. I'd been conducting my own campaign since Ezra was in middle school. Ezra had gotten sober a few months prior to Jean Luc's arrival, and I'd hoped my days of cohabitating with someone high on Pineapple Trainwreck were behind me.

Soon, whiskey took up residence next to his wine. This had a madeleine effect. The smell of the alcohol triggered remembrance of binges past. The bracingly medicinal odor was often the first fragrance I'd encounter in the morning, because I'd find half-full glasses en route to my first espresso. I began to worry that should I expire in my bedroom, I might not be discovered for months. Between the cigarettes, weed, bacon, and now whiskey, no one would notice the scent of my corpse decaying.

Neither sea monkey nor brine shrimp, I'd landed a frog, pickled and flambéed.

I was a bit confused by the binge-watching. Had he come all the way across the pond to watch the same shows you can stream worldwide? With his sad eyes and sulky countenance, I expected him to break out the Baudelaire or Rimbaud. But no, he was working his way through *The Office*, *Friends*, and *NCIS*—all of the cities, even Las Vegas. It didn't seem very French at all, it seemed so . . . American. When the speakers on his computer gave out, the situation was exacerbated. If there's an opposite of the bubbly chatter of an international artist colony, it's the sucking sound vacuum that is created when someone watches a comedy with headphones on, laughing at punch lines you can't hear.

Then the deadly wildfires of the winter of 2017 broke out. Up and down the California coast, the state was burning. Our neighborhood received a high fire risk warning, called a Red Flag Alert. During red flag conditions, residents are instructed to refrain from smoking or cooking outside, and to remove our cars from the narrower hillside streets, like mine, in case emergency response vehicles need to squeeze through on their way to a fire zone. I explained to Jean Luc that he'd need to stop smoking in the yard. He said he understood, but the next day, I noticed he was seated outside smoking weed. Was it possible he believed there was a weed exemption to the Red Flag Alert? I didn't know what to say. Instead, I placed an ashtray next to the couch and checked to make sure my homeowner's insurance was up to date.

Still, Jean Luc proved helpful around the house. My remaining cat's raison d'être was inviting rodents over for playdates. Pushkin toyed with them until he tired of their company, leaving them to roam freely about the house. I'm embarrassed to admit this, as I'm proud to call myself a feminist—if there were a card, I'd carry it— but I'd outsourced pest control to my ex. If my tenant hadn't been male, I might not have fallen into the habit of calling out his name upon spying one of Pushkin's playmates. "Jean Luc! Living room!" I'd yell and he'd race in, armed with a broom and dustpan. He never failed to dispense with them, although at times, his cool ease reminded me that the French had stood in the streets and welcomed Hitler when he rode into Paris.

Having a tenant also proved a reliable sleep aid.* Ever since I saw Brian DePalma's *Dressed to Kill*—in which a gamine, heavily lip-glossed Nancy Allen, circa 1979, strips down to her skivvies before realizing there's someone lurking in her bathroom—closing my eyes in a house alone has been problematic. I've since learned that many women, even those who aren't haunted by Allen's ear-piercing screams, have the same issue. My friend Suzette, whose husband Matt is a surgeon, confessed that since she ushered her fourth child out of the nest, when Matt is on call at night, she checks into a hotel. At times, I've relied on Xanax to fall asleep. When I weighed the choice of Xanax versus my tenant, there was no contest. Xanax knocks me right out, but it's addictive and has been linked to sleep eating and brain and memory impairment. The stain on the kitchen ceiling was spreading, resembling the wine region of

---

* I'd been so terrified of sleeping when my home emptied that I'd had the downstairs street-facing windows soldered shut.

Bourgogne; the skunky smell of cannabis clung to my clothing; but I was having no trouble engaging in my new pastime, mentally cataloging my tenant's shortcomings. Counting them like sheep sent me straight into REM sleep.

Friends inquired how it was going with my roomie.

"He's not my roommate, he's my tenant!" I insisted, determined to keep my boundaries. To my horror, a friend asked if Jean Luc was a potential "tenant with benefits."

"I'm probably the same age as his mother, and that's the last thing on my mind."

I focused my energy on trying to find the upsides to his residency. Every so often, I'd overhear him on the phone. When he was speaking French, I could imagine he was affirming what a marvelous choice Macron had made in choosing a wife twenty years his senior. But when speaking English, he'd be complaining about how his boss was a terrible businesswoman or some other stroke of bad luck that had befallen him, one of which was that his employer had cut his hours in half, which meant that he'd be spending only a few hours a day out of the house.

When Ezra came home for winter break, I assumed Jean Luc would make himself scarce, because what twenty-seven-year-old wants to hang with teenagers? This one. The house filled with Ezra's pals and I was elated to be cooking for the troops again, but now Jean Luc was eating my pancakes too. He was smoking and drinking with them in the backyard. Jean Luc's presence was so unremitting that one morning he joined us at the breakfast table and Ezra greeted him with "Hi Dad."

I weighed the pluses and minuses of having him at the house.

Plus	Minus
not murdery	too French
rent checks clear	too American
human Xanax	too actory
rodent wrangler	dogs follow me down the street
takes garbage out	strangers ask me directions to weed dispensaries
his binge-watching inspires me to watch less TV	
didn't say "hi" back when my kid called him dad	

The positives outweighed the negatives, but it was getting harder and harder to make eye contact. It shouldn't have been a surprise to see him every day, but it's like when I look at myself in a mirror. My mother's features began to overtake my own about five years ago, but each time I catch sight of myself, I'm stunned by how much I resemble her. Jean Luc would greet me in the morning by saying something patently criminal, like "Good morning," and I'd find it impossible to stretch my features into something resembling a warm smile. The best I could manage was a wan acknowledgment that he was still in residence.

What exactly was my breaking point? It's never one thing. Toward the beginning of spring, as the days grew longer, my patience grew shorter. One morning, I woke up to an email letting me know that an assignment I was counting on was not going to happen. This would mean more hemorrhaging from my savings account. I dragged myself into the kitchen to make a bracing double latte when Jean Luc bounded out of his room to question me about *Austin Powers*.

"*Austin Powers*? You want to talk about a movie?" I asked, wiping away my tears. He'd actually said Austin Pendleton, the actor. I hadn't heard him correctly.

"I've been dying to know if you like his work."

Although I am a big fan, there were few things less appealing at that moment than reviewing the highlights of Mr. Pendleton's career. It must have seemed like he'd interrupted the Grim Reaper pulling an espresso. Not one for reading social cues, he added that he'd been cast in a production of *The Importance of Being Earnest* and that he'd love for me to come. Any illusion of myself as a marginally good person evaporated when he added that it was being performed for kids with cancer. Normal etiquette dictates that you congratulate a person for entertaining sick children. Then, on the date of the show, you text, "So sorry! . . . stuck at work . . . traffic."* Instead, I mumbled an unintelligible sound, akin to the gurgling of someone being strangled.

But the last straw might have been the bathrobe incident. I'd been careful to always dress before entering our common areas, but one afternoon, thinking he wasn't home, I was fussing about the kitchen in a nightshirt. Really, it's more like papal regalia—the collar reaches high up on my neck and it covers my ankles. Jean Luc showed up to score his first bacon fix of the day. The next morning, he appeared for bacon-fast in a terry-cloth number that barely reached mid-thigh. It's like in a relationship, when you pee in front

---

* Why *The Importance of Being Earnest*, a comedy about the foibles of Victorian aristocracy, would be interesting to children with cancer is mystifying.

of someone the first time, it's hard to go backward. Now he was in that bathrobe all day long. It was a thigh too far.

I called my wise friend Claudia. After Claudia and her husband divorced, she was determined to keep the family house in case their three children boomeranged back home. She bought out her ex's share of the house, but now she was house-poor. After the kids left for college she rented out each of their bedrooms (during visits home they bunk in the finished basement room, once their playroom). She juggles a demanding job at the United Nations and as many as three tenants at the same time. I launched into my litany of complaints.

"Oh, honey," she sighed. "Everybody has at least one dud, deadbeat, drama queen or king, it comes with the territory. There was this one woman I couldn't get out of my house fast enough. She drank altogether too much and kept hitting on my Cuban boyfriend. She'd try and seduce him in Spanish, and the worst part was that her Spanish was dreadful. You should get rid of this guy. Also, have you sought out professional counseling?"

That's why she's my wise friend.

I worked up the courage to evict him only after lining up a new tenant. A friend of a friend needed a place to stay while writing on a TV show. He'd be working in a writers' room ten to twelve hours a day.

Jean Luc was in the backyard, in his spot, when I wandered over, pretending to admire a lemon the size of a baby's head ripening on the tree behind him. It was a Red Flag Alert day and he was smoking pot, which helped me maintain my resolve. I was nervous, but if he'd been tempted to off me, he'd had other opportunities.

"You know how we talked about six months? Well, I heard from a friend who needs a place to live and I told them they could move in," I lied. He gulped and looked up at me with those brooding, bloodshot eyes.

"I have to find a new place to live?"

"Yes. I'll help you!"

I offered everything short of packing his suitcase. We found him a bedroom in an apartment in the neighborhood. I gave a glowing reference to his new landlady, Lilliana, who hails from Normandy. I didn't mention to Jean Luc that she told me she'd had past tenants who'd cast voodoo spells and practiced black magic, red flags for crazy lady. I said nothing, because it wasn't any of my business, and he could do his own research. I like to imagine them taking hits on a bong and feasting on bacon-infused duck.

One of the lasting images I'm left with is of Jean Luc hunched over a cutting board carcassing a chicken to make bone broth. He said the most French thing I've ever heard. I asked him to pass me a package of rice cakes that were on the counter. He answered, "I don't know what that is."

Oh, Jean Luc, you thief. You stole my love of all things French, my fondness for bacon, the actor Austin Pendleton, and people who are twenty-seven years old. You took from me the illusion that I could change someone's luck. Bien sûr, you taught me things. I learned that ennui is just another word for being a bummer to be around.

I'm sorry, Jean Luc, *je regrette tout.* How must I have looked to you? Standing over the sink, shoving food in my mouth, like an animal.

They say you never forget your first, and I'll never erase the memory of you bending down to load the dishwasher in your tiny terry, no matter how hard I try. I think of you each time I attempt, unsuccessfully, to remove the nicotine stains on the bathroom walls, a souvenir of your surreptitious smoking. To cap things off, a few weeks after we said au revoir, a minor earthquake rattled both the pictures on the walls and my nerves. I cried, realizing it was the first time I'd been in danger when I wouldn't hear from my parents. My ex didn't phone to ask after my safety either, but you called and texted. Boy, did that make me feel like an asshole.

But, *mon ami*, you should have seen the denouement coming. Moving in with a middle-aged woman, in the process of getting divorced right after her only child goes off to college? There were plenty of red flags, Jean Luc. There were red flags.

The —— That Changes Everything

THE PILLOW THAT WAS GOING to change everything appeared to me in Des Moines.

It was February. I was halfway through a twelve-week national tour. The exchange of energy between audience and performer in live theater is my happy place, and a welcome break from the solitary life of a writer, but this was different. I'd accepted a touring schedule that required me to live out of a suitcase for three months. Even under the best of circumstances, every road warrior knows that at some point in your travels, rootlessness sets in. A fleeting loneliness can balloon into a bottomless well of existential dread that's tempting to fill with alcohol, sex, and Amazon Prime. One month on the road can lead to heavy drinking, two months to the breaking of marriage vows, and three months is why you read about comedians running naked through hotel hallways on drug-fueled escapades. This tour was going to let me bank five or six months of income and have enough left over to pay for that new couch. If I could just maintain my sanity and stick to a strict budget.

It helped that Diane, one of the theater staffers, was my Midwestern doppelganger. We had matching layered bobs, both of us were caring for aging parents, getting divorced, parenting teenagers, and juggling so many gigs that even our side hustles had side hustles. Audiences were giving the play a warm reception, and there was the additional and unexpected benefit of landing in Des Moines, the city known as the global hub of the insurance industry. Each day, I braved the cold to walk to work as the signage for Nationwide, Delta, Anthem, Cigna, and Blue Cross Blue Shield lit up the big western sky. On the hunt for lower premiums, I'd changed companies and plans so often that I'd tithed my income to all of these providers. It was like I was living the *Cheers* theme song: I'd landed in a place where everybody knew my name. Only my budget kept springing leaks.

I'd found a local yoga studio, but that still left eight hours before curtain time and a minimum of two or three more hours post-performance. I'd stay and chat with audiences after the show, but they had families to return to, as did Diane.

All day I'd try to avert my eyes from the "treat yourself" and "reward yourself" exhortations in shops and restaurants, or the "therapy is expensive, get a blowout instead" sandwich board outside the local hair salon. And each day I'd attempt some financial jujitsu. I didn't have champagne wishes and caviar dreams—I was aiming for happy hour house wine and grocery store sushi.

If I stick to the free breakfast buffet at the hotel every morning and sneak a couple of hard-boiled eggs and fruit salad in a container for lunch, then I get to have an Iowa-priced pinot noir nightcap at the hotel bar and dinner once a week at the restaurant with the theater discount.

But last night I had two glasses, so no nightcap tonight. Thelma's Bakery's signature snickerdoodles are sooooo delicious and I'm supporting a local business, so that's an essential. I have to go to yoga or I won't fit into my costume, so that's an essential too. Maybe I can sell an old DVF wrap dress on the RealReal?

But why did I buy that eighteen-dollar lavender-scented candle on the way to the theater? It makes the hotel room cozier and it isn't as expensive as the candle that smells like Gwyneth Paltrow's vagina, so I guess I saved money, but one candle equals a dinner out, which is equivalent to two salad bar dinners, or two nightcaps.

One afternoon, on a new route to the theater, I found myself in front of a Roche Bobois showroom window. I stopped in my tracks. If you're unfamiliar with this luxury brand retailer, their pricey sectionals resemble mattresses upon which every crayon in the world has melted. The signature Mah Jong line sits so low to the ground that their customer base must be people wealthy enough to have outsourced every activity, including standing up. I'd fantasized about sitting on those cushions, but was too intimidated by the Madison Avenue flagship store to go in. And then I saw it. In the middle of a sofa, shaped like a pincushion and the size of a baby hippo, a fuzzy pouf glowed like an iridescent marshmallow. It was as close to a religious experience as I've ever had—like seeing Mary Magdalene's face in a pancake. I stumbled inside, crawled across the sectional, wrapped my arms around the furry orb, and rested my head. This pouf would fill the gap left by my parents, kid, spouse, missing cat, dwindling savings.* Maybe I could take the stuffing out and have it injected into my face—it couldn't be more dangerous than the Botox I could no longer afford.

I didn't buy the pillow. It might have cost four figures. I'll never know because there was no price tag. I'd worked up the courage to walk into the store, and I visited it, like a puppy in a pet store window that your parents won't let you take home, but I was too intimidated to ask the price.

When I returned to Los Angeles, I couldn't stop thinking about the pillow that could change everything. I devoted time I couldn't afford to googling the pillow I couldn't afford before stalking knock-offs of it at Pier 1 and the slightly irregular as-is return pile at Crate and Barrel. My lust for comforting plushness expanded to fuzzy throws and rugs. Images of velutinous fabrics invaded every waking moment. They crept into my dreams. One night, I dreamed that I was enjoying a meal at a lively bar. Draped over the chair next to me was one of the velvety blankets I'd been eyeing. After my meal, I spread the blanket on the bar, stretched out, and went to sleep. You might think this would cause me to reconsider this mania, but no, I woke up thinking *gee, fun night out* and continued my quest.

The thing is, I've always been vigilant about not succumbing to the seduction of shopping. My father's appetite for the accoutrements of wealth came at a steep price—that was how we wound up with a both a Rolls-Royce Silver Cloud and a house in foreclo-

---

* As if all of that weren't enough, I got a call that Pushkin was happily spending his days with my neighbor who for the past few years, unbeknownst to me, has fed him breakfast and let him nap on his lap. I was second banana to my own pet!

sure. Before my sister stepped in to manage their affairs, our parents racked up credit card debt, had multiple mortgages, and owed $30,000 to their next-door neighbors, making their last years more aluminum than golden.

Another cautionary tale was seared into my memory. Leslie was a classmate whose family lived in a waterfront mansion so spare and elegant that an invitation to her home was like being granted a day pass to another dimension. The house was air conditioned like a meat locker, unlike ours, where fans often supplied the only relief from the punishing Floridian heat and humidity. After Leslie's parents divorced, the house took on the hushed atmosphere of a mortuary, but one day I noticed a pile of what seemed to be opened presents. In my memory, purses overstuffed with tissue paper were stacked, altar-like, in her mother's bedroom. Even then, I sensed something perverse about it. Twenty-five years later, newly reunited with Leslie through Facebook, I asked if I'd only imagined that scene. I hadn't. Her mother had gone on a shopping bender and was later required by court order to return them all.

Fear of this kind of penury had long kept me living not only within my means but well below it. My dedication to maintaining a low overhead is so well known among my closest friends that it earned me the nickname "The Squirrel."

But I'd discovered something even more addictive than that mood-lifting dopamine rush of the purchase: the exhilaration of checking off an item on my to-do list. With all the changes in my domestic life, including the loss of that organizing school year calendar, I was having trouble completing tasks. As every freelancer knows, if time management doesn't kill you, jumping through all the hoops to get paid can crush your soul. If I'm ever found slumped over my desk, I'd like the cause of my demise to be listed as "death by a thousand invoices." Shopping for pillows and throws became a task with a clearly defined beginning, middle, and end.

By the time I called my softness spree to a halt, I'd accumulated six fleecy throws, two faux sheepskin rugs, and ten furry pillows. It looked like a herd of alpaca were grazing in my living room.

Task completed. Check. Ms. Gurwitch will do her own shopping today.*

This kind of messaging was spoon-fed to my generation.† I was only eleven when Ilon Specht, then a twenty-three-year-old copywriter, penned that infamous L'Oréal tagline, "Because you're worth it!" The message was clear: spending more affirms self-worth.

As Jia Tolentino notes in her book *Trick Mirror*, women are regularly sold the idea that *something* can solve all your problems. *The look that changes everything. The brow, the bra, the diet, the workout, the yoga pant.* As an adolescent, I learned about the bath with magical powers.

A harried homemaker called out for release with the tagline "Calgon, take me away!" in those 1970s commercials. And wouldn't you know it, from frowsy to wowsy, flaxen locks piled high, she soaked in a tub the size of a station wagon. A long, luxurious bath, with the right water softener, could change everything. As a measure of just how completely my generation internalized this mes-

---

* Apologies to Virginia Woolf.

† In an interview for *The New Yorker*, Toni Morrison reflected on both the Black experience and consumerism: "We were called citizens . . . We were second-class citizens, but that was the word. And then, after World War II . . . they started calling us 'consumers.'"

saging, the Chicks (formerly known as the Dixie Chicks) have been quoted as saying that the Calgon slogan inspired their hit "Cowboy Take Me Away."

This trope was hilariously skewered in HBO's adaptation of Tom Perrotta's *Mrs. Fletcher.* Recent empty nester Mrs. F., portrayed by Kathryn Hahn, rolls her eyes at the women's-magazine entreaty to take to her tub for self-care. Cut to: she's not feeling the magic in her utilitarian tub and her single sad, overpriced (probably lavender-scented) candle. Spoiler alert: next thing you know, she's in the grip of a low-rent online porn addiction and then a real-life threesome that might best be described as Groupon Kink. If she hadn't fallen for that bath that could change everything, she might have taken up Zumba like every other empty nester.

I've ponied up for scrubs and salts in pursuit of the life-changing bathcation more times than I care to admit, and the outcome is reliable: my skin is that much drier than it was an hour earlier. Coincidentally, I've heard that the right moisturizer can change everything.*

If Wikipedia is to be trusted on this, the first reference to shopping as retail therapy appeared in a 1986 column penned by Mary Schmich in *The Chicago Tribune.* Schmich wrote, "We've become a nation measuring out our lives in shopping bags and nursing our psychic ills through retail therapy."†

It seems inevitable that women would be targeted through ad-

---

* Sylvia Plath once wrote, "There must be quite a few things that a hot bath won't cure, but I don't know many of them." That turned out not to be true.

† Schmich was clearly referencing T. S. Eliot's "I have measured out my life with coffee spoons."

vertisements to shop their way to happiness, as women have tra-
ditionally controlled the household purse strings—not to mention
that rewarding ourselves with little treats was one of few agencies
historically afforded to us. Even *Little Women*'s upright March sister,
Meg, is tempted by a shiny new object in the form of an expensive
bolt of fabric, but whew, she comes to her senses and exchanges it
for the winter coat her husband needed. The struggle is real!

In her book *You Play the Girl*, culture critic Carina Chocano re-
calls how she'd assumed her older friend was being overly simplistic
when she'd warned Carina, then in college and a determined as-
cetic, that she might be surprised by the pull of the constant sell.
"You walk down Madison Ave., you see things, eventually you start
to like them and then want them." Carina assumed her intellect
and education would inoculate her against falling into this trap,
which is why she was stunned to find herself splurging on nonessen-
tials and then swimming in debt just a few months after entering
the work world.

A YEAR AFTER ACCUMULATING ENOUGH cushy material to
line my own padded cell, I was working in Brooklyn for a month.
Each day, trundling from the friend's house where I was overstaying my welcome to the coffee shop where I was overstaying my
writing welcome, I noticed that nearly every woman in the neighborhood wore identical mustard-colored suede half boots and what
I think of as Huckleberry Finn pants. (Numerous editions of the
Mark Twain classic feature the main character attired in these
jeans on the cover.) Cut off at mid-calf and flared—allowing for the
funneling of freezing air to your thighs—they might be perfect for

fishing on the Mississippi, but are completely impractical for cold climes. Suede boots are also a mystifying choice in a rainy climate and for city life in general, where grime clings as unforgivingly as a bad review.

Tangentially, almost every bone-thin woman in this outfit was pushing a stroller, accompanied by at least one other child, and spooning ice cream. How do they stay that skinny? How many scoops of Lavender Olive Oil Stracciatella do you have to sell to make the pricey rent? That flavor is described as "grassy." Is there anyone who wakes up and thinks, *I'm craving grassy-flavored ice cream?* Just another unanswerable mystery of the gentrified boroughs of Brooklyn.

One day, I caught sight of yet another lollygagger, identically uniformed. It took me a full minute to realize I was gazing at my own image reflected in the Van Leeuwen shop window. I have zero recall of how this ensemble came to be on my person. I must have purchased it in a fugue state.

We don't need to leave our homes to be bombarded with "must-have purchases." Just this morning, I clicked onto a Facebook ad for a website selling that singular status symbol, the handbag. The site featured a troubling image: five strikingly dressed women teetering, side by side in precipitously high heels, in a lineup distressingly re-sembling a firing squad. Their faces were obscured by the purses they were clutching. Below the image, an announcement heralding the arrival (at long last) of a line from a coveted designer: "Finally, our prayers have been answered!"

Even the brightest woman I know, a biologist and big thinker, has a prodigious collection of pricey bags. The magical totems oc-cupy a small bedroom in her home and are displayed in modular shelving, illuminated like works of art. But who's getting the last laugh? *Forbes* tells us that a well-cared-for Birkin bag increases in value faster than gold.

It was like a dam had broken open. If I spent an entire day slogging through insurance EOBs, I might feel the need to reward myself with "the lipstick that every woman should own," but as every freelancer or person on a fixed income knows, the moment you think you might just be getting ahead and treat yourself to that lipstick, that's when you have *that* day.

The day you notice that there's an awful lot of lint building up inside your dryer. So you wrap some paper towels around a long bread knife because you're handy and you can clean it yourself, damn it, but the contraption slips out of your hand and now you've got to pay someone to take the machine apart, so you're googling "dryer duct cleaners" and you spill coffee on your computer. The good news is that your hard drive can be fixed and it will only cost $500 plus an extra hundred more if you need it fast-tracked, which you do because you thought you were saving everything to the cloud, but you weren't because you can't even figure out where the music you purchased is stored on your desktop. The bad news is that it takes two different service people to determine that you wedged the bread knife into the dryer's housing and you'll need to get a new machine. During the course of that day you lose your prescription glasses and, even though you're down to the drugstore reading glasses, which are not at all the same strength as your glasses, they work well enough to read the notice that the parking ticket that you got when you went on the interview for the job that you didn't get that was $25 is now $125. That's the day that you say, "Fuck it!" and you start borrowing from your future and spending down your retirement savings on hand-knitted sweaters for your pets.

I knew I had to break this obsession. My only hope was to seek solace in my community. Community is one of the few universally recognized spirit boosters that's achievable fully clothed. But my community was now hostage to the beguiling wares of Big Wellness.

Big Wellness isn't organized like the other "Bigs"—Big Oil or Big Tobacco. It doesn't have lobbyists or the infrastructure of Big Pharma, but it's every bit as insidious when it comes to preying upon the emotionally, physically, or financially vulnerable. With ambassadors as diverse as Gwyneth and the storefront tarot card reader, there's something for everyone and at every price point. For a few bucks you can buy crystals that "attract prosperity," or for a thousand—and that's just the entry fee—you can attend a Goop conference, where you can meet with the "intuitive psychic who has made millions with her superpowers" and wants to teach you how to do the same.*

Every morning I was deluged with emails from friends letting me know about all manner of "re": rekindling, recalibrating, reconnecting, reclaiming, resetting, and even "the law of self-restraint." I was initially intrigued, assuming self-restraint to be a form of BDSM that could be practiced solo; alas, it was only instruction for restricting your internet time. Other rejiggering included an invitation from another friend, now a Mojo Recovery Specialist, to reignite my unfettered access to "the money and the honey."

To assuage the worries of the financially strapped, one coach,

---

* As I wrote this, I found a card in the bottom of my purse. It says, "The red jasper stone provides a grounded flow of energy, vitality, enhanced memory and recall." Had I purchased a red jasper stone? Either I was "holding it for a friend" or bought it and lost it, but the red jasper's power must be dubious, because I can't remember purchasing or being given this stone, or what happened to it.

whose self-help tome is entitled *Pussy: A Reclamation*, offered a testimonial from a client saying something to the effect of, "I was afraid I couldn't afford to attend, but a friend offered to pay my way. I've reinvented my career and made back twice the cost of the seminar!"

I tracked down her business website. She's a money coach.

Exercise and yoga studios that once offered classes have rebranded as wellness collectives offering bonding experiences: "Come for the sound bath, stay for the chocolate tasting and social."

Just as brick-and-mortar stores were competing with online shopping by offering "experiences," friends were being recruited into sponsoring gatherings, circles, and salons at their homes. Almost every invite was ladies only.

A close friend regularly invites girlfriends to weekend retreats at a wellness center. The retreat includes yoga classes, two massages, and seven colonics. Typically, I respond with a note politely declining, but the last time I received this invite, I couldn't stop myself from replying, "I'd prefer to not spend the weekend surrounded by people who I know are spending the majority of their waking hours getting colonics."*

"Women are overrepresented, both as customers and consumers," Australian heart and lung surgeon Nikki Stamp characterized the wellness industry in the *Washington Post* in July 2019, as if she were privy to my email in-box. Why is that? "Women are more likely to have chronic illness and autoimmune diseases and become dissatisfied with the paternalistic and patriarchal medical industrial

---

* Both the Mayo Clinic and Johns Hopkins do not endorse colonics as necessary or even helpful to health.

complex," she explained in her pointed takedown of the healers featured in Amazon's *The Goop Lab* series.

Here's a completely anecdotal and unscientific example. During my peak earning years, and before switching to my industry health clinic, I was shelling out buckets of cash to a Beverly Hills GP. Struggling with depression and anxiety, I'd asked for a recommendation to a therapist. He pooh-poohed that idea, suggesting talk therapy with him instead. After a few minutes of listening to my woes, he told me that he had the cure. "Judd Apatow is a patient of mine. I could introduce you!"

I believe Dr. Show Business had the best of intentions, but not only had he broken doctor/patient confidentiality, which is illegal, he'd prescribed a male Hollywood power broker: take two meetings with Apatow and call me in the morning.

Even more promises of a brighter and more lucrative future are offered through teacher "certification" in all manner of "methodologies," including communicating with animals, self-compassion, and tarot card reading. The most craven was the chance to sample the secret sauce of Goop's money whisperer, who claims she "wants us all to be rich." Described in a *Forbes* profile as wisp thin, giddily in love with her spouse, and blessed with gorgeous and accomplished offspring (that claim alone must draw parents of millennials and Gen Z), the impeccably groomed financial wizard is pictured holding court surrounded by similarly well-heeled women. Her acolytes appear to hang on her every word, so much so that they are physically leaning in. As if to remind us that her $900 seminar will be fun, a cocktail glass is strategically positioned in the frame. In the *Forbes* profile, we learn that she has zero expertise in the industries she advises about and that her confidence in calling up the right answer to even the most pressing decisions is unequivocal.

We'd be attending a workshop that promises to turn everyone into my mother.

It was in no way remarkable to see *Vice* declaring that we'd reach "peak astrology" in 2019. Still, it made my heart sink as a measure of our nation's collective uneasiness. I had the same reaction to the Women's March of 2019. I carried a sign that read: I THOUGHT I WAS DONE MARCHING FOR THIS.

Astrology's twenty-first-century rebirth has a digital spin, with zodiac dating sites geared to "manifesting rising sign compatibility" and Instagram's zodiac filter, which adds neon star sign symbols to your selfies. I'd been intrigued, mistakenly assuming it would filter *out* anything that mentioned astrology.

"Come over and help me celebrate my new home!"

That was the subject line of an email I received from a newly divorcing friend. Only it wasn't merely a housewarming. An astrologer was coming to give us a glimpse into how the stars were lining up—and for forty dollars, we'd each get a ten-minute private reading. We'd need a commitment of at least fifteen people to make it worth her time.

After being assured it was cool to come and not get the reading, I discovered that the astrologer was a former colleague at a respected newspaper who'd recently reinvented herself. Look no further for grim confirmation of "peak astrology." Instead of parsing more wonky data on the economic insecurity of the middle-aged, news organizations could simply publish this sentence: "The astrologer was formerly a highly respected freelance journalist who concluded in the summer of 2019 that she would earn more doing horoscopes at women's soirees."

A gathering guaranteed to bring your crew closer, her website describes her services . . . and she delivered. We oohed and aahed as her PowerPoint presentation described happenings terrestrial and celestial. I objected to the slide that featured Michelle Obama, a Capricorn, with the tagline "When they go low, we get our charts done!"

I just made that up. Her presentation was witty and whimsical, *and it was fun.*

Still, we could have played charades or a board game because forty dollars isn't an insignificant sum; for that much I'd like to have something to show for it, even a mani-pedi. As these things tend to go, the evening was also an "upsell," to use multi-level-marketing speak, for her weekly coaching services.*

While I want to support my sisterhood, I can't help but worry about the vulnerable soul, emotionally, physically, financially (or all three) desperate for the inside scoop on that holiest of grails—"the timing for when life things get better." This is the astrologer's promise on her website, and her clients (according to the endorsements on the site) take her word as gospel. But who am I to pass judgment? I'm a Scorpio and everyone knows we are overly opinionated.

I returned home from the housewarming, swaddled myself in a fleecy throw, and pondered that chicken-and-egg conundrum: Were journalists becoming readers because the end is near, or do journalists becoming readers portend the end of the world?

---

* I recommend door-to-door voter registration as a great low-cost way to catch up with a friend.

I called my sister, the cerebral CEO, who seemed to have rebounded after feeling stymied by some challenging issues. She told me she'd seen her corporate coach—a licensed therapist who works with numerous high-powered corporate officers.

"What kind of work does that coach do with you?"

"Sometimes we talk through proven leadership strategies. Or talk through a course of action and play out scenarios with different outcomes."

Then she said that prior to a recent session, she'd received some upsetting news. She'd been crying when she arrived, so the coach invited her to stretch out on the office couch. She covered her in a blanket and tucked her in.

"Was this one of those weighted anti-anxiety blankets?"

"No."

"Was it blessed by the Dalai Lama? Did she have you hold a crystal close to your heart?"

"Nope."

"So, so she tucked you in with . . . a blankie? How was it?"

"Amazing."

Is that what we're heading toward? A nation of Linuses dragging our blankies behind us?

Blankies? I am prepared.

If You Lived with Me You'd Be Home by Now

THE FIRST FEW NIGHTS THEY spent under my roof I couldn't sleep. I stashed the closest thing I could find to a weapon, a rusty hatchet, under my bed. A tetanus infection was the most damage I could cause with a blade this dull. Why had I invited two homeless strangers and their bunny rabbit into my house?

By the spring of 2019, so many tenants had come and gone that the cat had almost doubled in size, what with the extra snacks from boarders who'd fallen under his spell. There was the writer who made us omelets and wore wide-brimmed straw hats indoors. Austen from Austin, the college student with a smile that lit up a room like a glitter bomb, who left the house cleaner than when she arrived. The recent divorcé who greeted me each morning with a rousing "We're going to crush it today." The lesbian lovebirds whose terrier peed on my favorite rugs—they'd also broken the front door lock, the bathroom sink, and the dishwasher. But all in all, it was revitalizing and provided a steady source of income.

Hosting the couple and the Jersey Wooly dwarf bunny was not plan A, B, or even C.

A few months before taking to my bed with a hatchet, I'd participated in the citywide annual homeless count. I'd volunteered because I was disappointed in myself. "Do they really need to bunk right out in the open? They're hurting our businesses," I'd thought, sidestepping an expansive homeless encampment in front of my favorite wine bar. Us? Them? When did I become that person? I was one of two hundred locals who assembled at 9:00 p.m. on a school night at the Hollywood City Hall.* Diverse in every way imaginable, our number included gym rats, middle-aged women wearing *Roe v. Wade* forty-four-year commemorative pins, young people beaming with the ecstatic idealism of political canvassers, and elderly activists sporting well-worn AmeriCorps T-shirts.

"Treat everyone you encounter as if you're visiting friends in their living rooms after a long, hard day," instructed local city councilman David Ryu, adding, "Your safety is pandemonium." What might have been an embarrassing malapropism drew no laughter, perhaps because we were contemplating his most thought-provoking suggestion. When looking for the "unsheltered," we were to ask ourselves, *If I were sleeping outside, where would I be?*

We were paired up and issued flashlights, yellow vests, and official-looking clipboards. Then, in an act of faith that defies social convention, we hopped into vehicles driven by our (un-vetted) fellows who, moments prior, were complete strangers. Soon, I was one of four local moms in a minivan, snaking our way through Hollywood.

---

* The visual count is conducted at night to get the most accurate snapshot of who is sleeping unsheltered. In 2018, 17,000 city residents took part in the count.

Our survey tract, which we were to canvass on foot, included Gardner Street, the same street where I'd made my home when I arrived in 1989 to pursue acting work. I lived in the neighborhood for seven years and I thought I knew the area well, but the city appears vastly different when looking for a place to bed down for the night.

Behind the hedges of a quaint apartment building? Too dark and secluded, making me vulnerable to robbery or rape. Could I rest on the front porch of that craftsman bungalow and wake before anyone noticed? Too risky: I might be mistaken for an intruder.

It was midnight when we tallied our last soul, a total of seventeen, but we were sure we'd missed folks. It was particularly challenging to determine if someone was living in a car.* A late-model sedan crowded with shopping bags, an assortment of takeout containers in the back seat? That could have been my car, except for the blanket draped across the back windshield. Before we parted, I asked my counting buddy what she would do if things ever spiraled down for her. "I guess I'd go back home," she whispered. A thudding reality set in. Having spent more than half of my life in the city, there was no longer anywhere to go back to. This city was my "back home."

A month later, I was sitting in traffic when my ears perked up. Marlene and Michael Rapkin were speaking about "walking the walk" of their social justice values in an interview on NPR. They spoke about their commitment to "welcoming the stranger." This phrase refers to the Old Testament account of Jewish enslavement

---

* Accurate reporting is necessary because funding for the unhoused depends on knowing how many people need services, much like the census.

in ancient Egypt. As I understand it, the remembrance that "we were once strangers in the land of Egypt" compels us to empathize with all who are experiencing injustice and oppression. It was in this spirit that the Rapkins had welcomed a housing insecure couple into their home for three months as part of a trial rapid rehousing program for young people between the ages of eighteen and twenty-four. It sounded like a tremendously rewarding experience and one that I'd never take on personally. I am that do-gooder who works in soup kitchens, marches, and campaigns for causes, but I didn't have the means to afford this kind of gesture. Also, opening my home? I wasn't that good. But when my next tenant canceled with little notice, on a lark, I looked up the program the Rapkins had talked about and learned that it provided a small monthly stipend. It wouldn't be as much as I'd been pulling in, but it was something.

Safe Place for Youth's (the sponsoring organization, which goes by the initials SPY) host-vetting process involved background checks and a home inspection. From what I'd seen online, the other local hosts had more spacious abodes and updated kitchens, so I worried my home wouldn't meet their standards, but the inspection was actually conducted to confirm that you don't have a dungeon in your basement or needlepoint samplers of swastikas or gay conversion pamphlets lying around.* Of course, if you had those items in your possession, you'd put them away before the inspection, right? Thankfully, the walk-through didn't include an assessment of my marginal housekeeping skills.

---

* Home sharing is an old-world tradition, but this incarnation of Host Home programs was started in London, thirty years ago, to support LGBTQ+ youth.

At the training for potential hosts, we received coaching in active listening, and we role-played potentially triggering interactions. "What are you doing today?" might sound like "You should be doing something productive!" Better to say "Good morning, nice to see you," and allow your houseguest the choice of continuing the conversation. After the trauma of being unsheltered, our houseguest might simply need to rest. As hosts, we'd be expected to embrace the core values of the program model including this awareness: "We understand that youth will sometimes make choices we don't agree with, and we acknowledge the youth's right to make those choices for themselves." Also, that "there are typically a variety of factors contributing to housing insecurity, many happen through no fault of their own."

We weren't signing on to assume a parental role but to provide positive role modeling and a safe space for our houseguests to evaluate next steps with their housing case manager.

We were invited to a picnic that was not unlike a Match.com mingle for the unhoused. SPY believes that the most successful host-houseguest matches were ones based on mutual common interests. Stations were set up in SPY's community garden to encourage casual conversation. These included a drum circle, harvesting herbs from the garden to create calming elixirs, and guided meditation. This was Los Angeles, after all.

I recognized potential hosts from the training—they had that deer-in-the-headlights look, like me. There were dozens of young people milling about, and a buffet overflowing with cheeses, freshly baked breads, and lentil salad. I wasn't planning on eating because I didn't want to take food from people living on the street, but there were creamy lemon bars with a crumbly graham cracker crust, topped with edible flowers. I snuck one or two, or seven, into my handbag. Honoring my austerity budget, I hadn't eaten anything that I hadn't prepared myself in months. Edible flowers, who could resist?

While chatting up a young person savoring the last bites of a lemon bar, I figured our mutual appreciation of dessert was enough of a reason to warrant an invitation.

"Would you like to come live at my house?" I stammered.

"Gee, thanks, Annabelle, but it's me, Andrew, and I have a place to live." I was so nervous that I hadn't recognized him as the social worker who'd led my training session.

He gestured toward two youths near the beverages. "That's Keyawna and Jesse, two SPY members [as the youth are described]. I saw you speaking with them earlier." Just then, the adorable bunny rabbit Keyawna was holding leapt from her arms and she dashed off to retrieve it. We'd shared some fruit punch. They'd mentioned that the bunny had a following on Instagram and they wanted to get the rabbit an agent so it could work in commercials. I'd nodded supportively but thought, *I can't book a commercial, but good luck!*

I'd moved on quickly because they looked . . . sketchy. Both of their faces were inked. She had the word CURED stamped in bold block lettering on one cheek and a wildflower on the other. I associate facial tats, even flowers, with drugs and gangs. Plus, there were two of them. I wouldn't feel safe being outnumbered. It might increase my water bill. Besides, my cat Pushkin thinks anything furry is dinner.

"Anyone but them," I said.

"Are you sure you can't take this couple? They're living in their car."

"I'm positive."

But that night, I lingered in the guest bedroom. *"Where would I sleep if I were outside?"* I asked myself. Keyawna and Jesse had been living—sweltering—in their 2008 Kia. With a rabbit. It seemed wrong to have an empty bedroom with 4,800 youths on the street and approximately 15,748 Angelenos living in their vehicles, as I'd learned doing the count. *Why did I have to know these things?* "Stop listening to NPR," I needed to immediately warn friends. (It was on my local station that I'd heard about the Host Home program and signing up for the homeless count.) I called SPY and a coffee date was arranged, the next step toward home sharing.

At the café, Andrew suggested that the three of us had a lot in common. "Keyawna is a rapper and Jesse is a tattoo artist. You're all in the arts." I wasn't buying it. Jesse and I agreed that hot coffee was vastly superior to cold caffeinated drinks, but we were not in the same arts. They hoped to become influencers on YouTube and TikTok, and I was in the real entertainment business. There was something about them that seemed familiar: their clunky, vaguely orthopedic, thick-soled shoes. What we called, back in the day, clodhoppers. Ezra wore those same dad sneakers.

I pay close attention to footwear. This habit dates back to my twenties when I worked at an infamously louche New York City nightclub. Nell's on Fourteenth Street was the kind of place where you could reasonably expect to snort cocaine off a stranger's clavicle any time between eleven at night and four in the morning, any night of the week. I was part of the door crew, charged with deciding who gained entry. The staff was composed of former classmates from NYU. Someone was hired and they told two friends, and they told two friends; we were living examples of that 1970s Herbal

Essences shampoo campaign.* One of the more experienced staff members insisted that footwear was a reliable barometer of social status. Shoes didn't need to be expensive, per se, just expressive. For instance, someone wearing ballet slippers, which happened more often than you'd have predicted, I waved in.

Based on my implicit shoe bias, I invited Keyawna and Jesse into my household.

The morning of their arrival, I got up at six. I scrubbed and scoured their bathroom, laid out my fluffiest towels, made their bed with my highest-thread-count sheets, and placed fresh flowers in their room. Then I hid my jewelry and my grandmother's sterling silverware in my bedroom closet, unearthed the rusty hatchet from the garage, stashed it under my pillow, and tested out the lock on my bedroom door.

I'd bought bagels and fruit as a welcome gift, and I'd intended to say "Eat anything you want," but I spotted a New York strip steak in the freezer, the last cut of pricey beef that an aunt sends for my birthday every year. I did not want to share that. Besides, they might feel obligated to replace the steak, and I couldn't expect them to spend that kind of money. If I told them that I hadn't purchased it myself and it was a present so could they please not eat it, it might sound like I was making it up. I also didn't want to emphasize our income disparity by flaunting my rich people food, because that might put a wedge between us and lead to class warfare in my

---

* The first person hired was Nicole Burdette, now a well-established playwright and professor at the New School. Other colleagues included Paul Eckstein and Chris Brancato, who teamed up after manning the door to executive produce television programs. Among their successes is the popular *Narcos* on Netflix.

kitchen, which would result in my murder. But where could I hide a frozen steak, except in my stomach? So, at 6:30 a.m., I cooked the meat and shoved the whole thing in my mouth because they were due any minute. I opened every window to air the house out because I didn't want to upset them with my rich people food smell.

My houseguests were over two hours late. *They're irresponsible,* I thought. "Unorganized," I texted my friend Judith, who reminded me that I'd once been three hours late for a lunch date.

As I showed them around the house, I offered up the story of how, in a fit of anger, I'd stepped out of the shower, naked and sopping wet, and kicked Ezra's bedroom door down when they'd come home obviously stoned. Was I putting them on notice that I was a take-no-prisoners badass? Maybe. I heard Keyawna whisper "I fucking love you" under her breath, which I took to be a good sign.

We negotiated a personal conduct contract that included cleaning the kitchen after usage, no alcohol or illegal drugs in the home, and SPY's standard prohibition against weapons. "I won't ask you to do anything I won't be doing," I assured them. I noticed that Jesse was rubbing his eyes and looked like he was about to nod off. Did he have ADHD? Was he on drugs? Was that why they were experiencing homelessness? "Keep the bunny in his hutch," I cautioned when the cat sauntered in, attracted by the scent of rabbit.

I wanted them to know that I trusted them, which I absolutely did not, so an hour after they arrived, I left for a yoga class. As I walked out the front door, I heard Keyawna singing in the shower. She had really good pitch. I could just make out the lyrics "I hate all . . . people." That couldn't be good.

When I arrived home, Keyawna and Jesse were relaxing in the living room, exactly as I'd invited them to do. She was darning socks and he was drawing on a sketchpad. "I'm so glad you're making yourselves at home," I said, and they smiled sweetly at me. But I was thinking, *Are they sweating homeless people sweat into the Rhoda?*

That night, my houseguests got their much-needed rest while I anxiously sat vigil in my bedroom, located directly above the guest room, listening for noises until the sun rose, drinking wine, having broken our contract within ten hours of their arrival. I was spiraling into worrisome dilemmas. My wood-framed stucco house carries sounds like a boat, so the hollow click of the flimsy lock on my bedroom door might upset them, inspiring some kind of Charles Manson-y retaliation, so in addition to having that rusty hatchet within arm's reach, I opened the windows and the door to a Juliet balcony off of the bedroom in case I needed to shimmy down a tree and make a quick escape.

As the days progressed, my guests occupied themselves with suspicious activities like sewing, drawing, and reading books. My inner circle fretted for my safety. "Text me before you go to bed," one urged. "Texts will just provide a timeline for your murder," another chimed in. I made light of my fears by keeping a running tally: "It's been twenty-four hours and my house hasn't burned down," or "It's been seventy-two hours and I'm still breathing!"

I was showering at my yoga studio to save money on the water bill, siphoning shampoo and rinse from the studio's supplies, and, even though I'd committed to upholding SPY's values, I was looking for clues as to why Keyawna and Jesse were experiencing homelessness. Meanwhile, my houseguests prepared salads, unloaded the dishwasher (unprompted), fed the predatory cat, called their mothers, joined the congregation of a church, and even locked me out of the house, not realizing I was in the backyard, in an effort to keep my home secure.

We began having meals together. They didn't owe me their story, but after a week under my roof they were eager to share it. They hailed from Beaver County, Pennsylvania, which has one of the highest opioid addiction rates in the nation. One in five children grow up in poverty, and employment opportunities are mostly limited to the fracking industry and a local steel mill. "It's just bars and angry husbands," Keyawna said of her hometown. They'd left after the only cultural hub, the local mall, was razed to make way for yet another fracking site.

Since founding SPY in 2011, Alison Hurst has seen a marked difference in the youth on the streets. In the past, they might have been "footloose travelers," but now they're "children of the working poor." This was true of my houseguests. One of their families' homes was in foreclosure; they'd endured periods of time when the water and power had been shut off; their childhoods cut short by caring for siblings; transiency; and Keyawna had a sibling whose chronic health conditions strained the family's resources.

Both Keyawna and Jesse had attended a year of college and had then forfeited college scholarships, partly out of a desire to contribute more quickly to their families' strained finances and partly because they'd been shuttled into career paths that didn't interest them. Keyawna was on track to become a parole officer; Jesse was sent to a college to become a dental hygienist because of his steady hands, which is how he wound up becoming a tattoo artist. Convinced it was their destiny to become artists, they'd saved up money to move to Los Angeles.

Neither knew a single person in Los Angeles, but from the

moment they arrived, Keyawna was making money working as a personal assistant, housesitting, networking at venues she'd seen on YouTube, eating healthily, and exercising. She'd been hired by her seatmate on the plane, a music producer. The girl had charisma and chutzpah to burn.

The facial tattoos, which I'd considered a terrible limitation to employment opportunities, were not an uncalculated move. Lil Nas X, Lil Mosey, Lil Uzi Vert, Lil Xan . . . all the Lils, the big names in the scene they wanted to join, have them. They'd gotten the tattoos just prior to their arrival in town. Producers would see them and comment, "nice face." Her talent plus their distinctive body art was getting her music noticed, and Jesse was earning money tattooing people in that crowd.

Jesse had designed the MORE LOVE inked in florid script above Keyawna's brow. As we talked, Jesse took off his skater beanie for the first time since we'd met and I saw that his tattoo, in matching font, read LESS HATE. Up until then, the hat had obscured the word "Less" and all I'd seen was "Hate." That was a relief.

Things had fallen apart for them, "through no fault of their own," as I'd learned at my training but suspected wasn't true. Without community ties, unused to big city life, with little time for any due diligence and spotty internet access, they fell victim to a number of scams, shady landlords, and price-gouging at motels. It's people who can least afford it who are often ripped off, because time itself is a privilege. The majority of their clothing and possessions were stolen at a hostel. They were robbed at gunpoint. Twice.

A character in Hemingway's *The Sun Also Rises*, when asked how he went bankrupt, answers, "Gradually and then suddenly." He might have been writing about Keyawna and Jesse. They were couch surfing and spending the occasional night in the car. Gradually, the number of nights spent in the car outnumbered the nights under a roof. One day, they ran out of couches. Suddenly, they were living in their car.

The ten days prior to moving into my home had been miserable. They'd unknowingly parked for the night near a trap house (a place where illegal drugs are sold), and someone had broken into the car and attacked Keyawna while they slept. After that, they were so freaked out they stayed awake each night until daybreak, napping briefly when the sun rose, so they could spend their days productively. They hadn't had a shower in ten days when they'd shown up at my front door.

I'd assumed they were irresponsible and unorganized because they'd turned up late on the day they moved in, but their day began at six, just like mine.

They'd stopped at a Jack in the Box, their usual spot, for a sponge bath with baby wipes so they would show up smelling fresh. Next, they'd emptied out a storage unit they could no longer afford. Then they'd tried their hand at DoorDash.

Everything, from small tasks like signing onto DoorDash to receiving services through local and state-run agencies, was made harder by being on the move daily, the constant search for bathrooms, affordable food, outlets to charge the phone.

Registering with the food delivery app was rife with impediments. Jesse had an outstanding juvenile misdemeanor on his record. He'd been charged with "internal possession of marijuana." He'd tested positive while working on a factory line in Utah. These charges were being expunged from young people's records, but prior experience with the juvenile justice system meant he was wary of attempting to rectify this situation. It was the kind of thing that a parent with just a bit more time than his parents, who both work long hours, might have dispatched quickly. The upshot was that they registered with DoorDash under Keyawna's name, only she couldn't afford car insurance, so she registered as a bicycle Dasher.* Their first order came in: a strawberry slushie from Carl's Jr.

Here's where it got even more tricky. Drivers are required to photograph the receipt for each order and send it to the app, but the camera on Keyawna's phone was on the fritz, so they arranged to meet up with a friend with a better phone. Once they had a working camera, they snapped a picture of the receipt and were heading to make the delivery when they were notified by DoorDash that receipts must be sent from the location where the orders are filled. They turned around and drove back to Carl's Jr., but by then the phone battery had died (they didn't have a working charger in the car). They charged the phone at the restaurant, snapped a picture, and by then, the friend needed the phone back ASAP because they gig for Postmates. So, back to the friend, and finally they were able to make the delivery. The slushie was melted, but they knew they wouldn't be receiving a tip because the customer was ten years old. They'd earned exactly two dollars. And were responsible for their own gas and wear and tear on the vehicle. Thus, they were late for the move-in. That all these things had happened, and they still believed in God, might be the most remarkable part of their story.

"Why don't they just get full-time service jobs?" a friend asked.

---

* The practical effect of this is that bicycle orders are smaller, making it that much harder to earn money, just another way that this system is rigged against vulnerable people earning commissions and tips.

Ironically, I'd just thrown in the towel on attempting to get my kid a summer dishwashing job.

The more I got to know about their lives, the more that phrase, "through no fault of their own," kept floating through my head. They'd chosen to come here. But there weren't opportunities to pursue careers in the arts in their hometown, and if our society can't accommodate artists from diverse backgrounds, that would mean only the privileged get to be artists, and that didn't seem right either.

Early one morning, Keyawna sought me out. She was worried that she and Jesse had broken the "conflict-free zone" clause in our contract by arguing in the house the night before. I assured her that I hadn't heard them. I'd seen no reason to worry for her safety, so I listened and offered the same advice I'd give to my own kid. "Take a breath, go for a walk in nature, and don't feel you need to solve everything today." After dispensing what I considered pretty sage advice, I headed out to indulge in some moderately low-cost self-care. It wasn't until the second coat of Yummy Mummy was being applied to my toes that I remembered what Rachel Pedowitz, who'd overseen SPY's Host Home launch, had warned: "When you're housing insecure you are always dealing with pressurized situations. Every single decision is around survival." Had I inadvertently advocated for ending the relationship? That might destabilize their already shaky support system. Taking stock and renegotiating terms is a regular and arguably important feature of any relationship, but self-care, privacy, even a breakup and make-up sex are luxuries not afforded to the housing insecure.

By the end of that week, Ezra returned from college. Would Ezra be inspired to drop out of school, get tatted up, and chuck their sobriety? Ezra was two and a half years sober, and although my houseguests had agreed not to smoke weed or drink alcohol in my home, I knew it was a regular feature of their lives. Would there be some kind of culture clash? My anxiety was unfounded; by the end of that second week, my formerly empty nest was filled with music, chatter, and dad sneakers as the three of them blended together.* Pushkin claimed two lizards, a baby possum, a bird, and a rat, but the bunny was still alive, which represented yet another of my questionable assessments.

The couple hadn't anticipated the lack of permanent housing when they'd adopted Appa (named for the magical monster in *Avatar: The Last Airbender*, the Nickelodeon series, which Ezra and I had loved as well). Caring for Appa grounded them, and they were constantly improving their "bunny parenting" skills. How many times had I harshly judged those experiencing homelessness with pets, never imagining that their animal companions entered their life prior to losing their home and might represent their last vestige of stability?

At the start of the third week, their friend, the local rapper who went by Sketchy, suffered an overdose and died. Even though I am the parent of a child in recovery from addiction, I said to myself, *Well, that's what happens when you travel in these circles. It's unsurprising.* Two days later, a friend of Ezra's died from an overdose. Then I discovered that Sketchy's parents and I had friends in common. Andrew was right; we were more alike than I could have imagined. Now the three of us were united in grief.

As we grieved these losses, Jesse asked if he could show me

---

* I had one hard and fast rule: I told Ezra that I wouldn't pay for college if they got a tattoo, and here I'd invited someone who did tattoos to live with us, but when Ezra returned to school, the number of tattoos stayed the same.

a picture of his parents. A middle-aged couple, dressed for some happy occasion, their smiles wide, faces beaming with love, they looked exactly like the parents I'd sold cupcakes with at Walter Reed Middle School's Jazz Band B fundraisers. "In case you wanted to know," Jesse explained, and I knew what he meant. In case I wasn't already convinced that he was someone who was loved and was capable of loving. I'd bounced around a lot when I first moved to town but had never felt compelled to demonstrate my humanity by showing a picture of my parents to anyone who hosted me.

I then did something that, up until that point, I'd been too fearful to do. I put their names into Google and held my breath. My search pulled up a site that gathers personal information through public records. Jesse scored 3.7 out of a possible 5 points, earning him a "fair" character assessment. He was flagged for possible civil court records. Fair? That didn't sound good. To get perspective, I entered my own name. I scored even lower than he did, with 3.5 points. A blinking RED ALERT accompanied my name. Court records! Civil cases! Bankruptcies! There was a sketchy person in the house, and that person was me.

It was then that I abandoned every last "us" and "them" I'd been clinging to. My guests seemed like regular people because they were regular people, and one in ten regular young people in America experience homelessness during a given twelve-month period.

Was it dumb luck that had kept me treading water when I was their age? Or was it my superior talent? Or both? That was the story I told myself for years: I'd single-handedly overcome my chaotic childhood.

Just as many factors had contributed to Keyawna and Jesse's being unsheltered, many factors had contributed to buoying me up when I landed in L.A. My wide social network, developed when I'd worked at Nell's in New York, connected me with a lucrative part-time hostessing gig when I first arrived in Los Angeles. Entry-level acting jobs, while not easy to score, were attainable. These supporting best friend roles were typically cast with girls who could deliver the funny, which was code for "could be Jewish or Black." These paid well and came with health care and pension contributions, but perhaps even more importantly, all of these jobs helped strengthen our community and that all-important social network. Keyawna and Jesse were subject to the vagaries of the gig economy, in which not only is the monetary compensation uncertain, but how do you build any kind of camaraderie in isolation, recording TikTok videos in your bathroom or delivering slushies to prepubescents?

The connections I made during those early years were so numerous that when I arrived in town, I slept in guest bedrooms, couches, and even floors—but there was always another place to stay.

The rent on my first place, a sunny studio apartment in a well-maintained building, was $750 a month in 1989. Studios average $1,500 in the area now, and since wages haven't kept up, it's no wonder that *The Hollywood Reporter* did a story in 2019 about gainfully employed young people in the entertainment industry who are living in their cars and vans.

There was one other significant difference in our backgrounds, and it's the one that had the biggest impact on our paths.

The zip code where you grow up turns out to be a major determinant of how much money you'll make in your lifetime.* If you're raised in Charlotte, North Carolina, you've got a 4 percent chance of bettering the circumstances of your birth, but in San Jose, California, a 13 percent shot at it. It doesn't matter if your family of origin are high earners, and it's not just the better school systems you get to attend—it's also having access to people who have access to wealth.

Like Keyawna and Jesse, I'd funded my move to Los Angeles with savings too. Only they'd worked for a year, doing manual labor jobs to earn their way, while I'd cashed in stocks that I'd been given for my bat mitzvah, not from my own family (we didn't have those kinds of resources) but from a family friend. The zip code they grew up in did not provide access to that kind of connection.

This is the biggest benefit of the home-sharing model and why it makes sense to have supportive bridge and low-income housing integrated into more affluent neighborhoods. Living in a stable environment where you are exposed to positive role models can create ripple effects. If we had housing like that in my neighborhood, Keyawna and Jesse wouldn't have been strangers, just neighbors I hadn't met yet.

During their last days under my roof, Ezra and Jesse worked together to repair the damage caused by Appa's (adorable) nibbling on my floor moldings. I invited Keyawna into my bedroom closet to ferret out clothing for a music video she was shooting. And just like

* Zip code data has been widely reported by Pew and other organizations. American University professor Jessica Owens-Young's essay for BlueZones.com includes this statistic: just ten miles in America can represent a life expectancy difference of almost thirty-three years.

that, every boundary I'd made was crossed. If only I'd filmed her reactions as she humored me while I suggested various items of my clothing. She's a terrific actress. Standing next to the silver and jewelry, still in the closet, she confided that she was just a bit psychic. "I knew you'd like us" from the minute we met, she said. I didn't have the heart to tell her that she'd been mistaken when she settled on an outfit, an old torn slip—very Patti Smith.

The night they left, I found a note thanking me for giving them hope. I sent them off with a bag stuffed with the collection of samples I've pilfered from hotel stays. But not all of them, not the Le Labo Rose 31 body lotion—I'm not crazy! That stuff is like crack.

With Appa no longer in the house, Pushkin calmed down, and the avian and small mammal kill rate in my neighborhood has thankfully decreased. Bits of pulpy bunny litter have permanently lodged in the nooks and crannies of my home, just as my default otherizations and incorrect assumptions have been indelibly transformed. As television writer Lijah Barasz—who, along with her husband Wes High, were among SPY's first hosts, and who offered coaching during my tenure—put it, "I don't think I'm very special, I'm not under any illusion that I'm solving the problem. When I told friends what I was doing, it seemed extraordinary, but now, after having this experience, it seems like the most normal response."

My houseguests moved on to another Host Home, waiting for that much sought-after affordable housing to open up, and three months later it did. Six out of the six youths of SPY's inaugural year were placed in permanent housing. I was only the seventh household to participate in the program and the first one of the second crop of hosts to be matched. Somehow, I hadn't known the numbers when I got involved; I assumed there had been hundreds before me. I can't say I would have done it, had I realized.

We have stayed in touch.

After they moved into their apartment, which I visited to drop off housewarming gifts, I received an email from a friend who'd remembered my change in marital status. She had a couch that needed a new home. If only she'd reached out before I'd purchased the Rhoda. This couch would be too large for Keyawna and Jesse's place, but a gentleman caller happened to be in the market for that exact size and style sofa, and the savings would be welcome. The couch went to his home and his old sofa was delivered to their new place. We extended not only the social network, but the sofa network.

Last year, we celebrated Keyawna's and my birthdays together with a picnic. We were born two days, thirty-seven years, and many zip codes apart.

We shut Pushkin in my bathroom so Appa could run around the backyard. They gave me career updates and I tried to listen without judgment. Her managers told her when she gets enough of a following on social media, they will get her paying gigs. "What's the threshold that translates into making money?" I asked. She wasn't sure. It seems a bit sketchy, but I have learned to smile and say, "It sounds like you are feeling good about how it's going." I try not to be attached to an outcome for them. I don't know if she'll make it as a rapper or he'll become an artist of note. I didn't mean to give them hope! A life in the arts is filled with constant rejection, financial insecurity, and disappointment. I never encourage anyone to go into the arts, especially people I care about. I wish they'd do something else, anything else, but youth often make choices that we don't approve of. Youth is one privilege they have, and hopefully they will have time to make many choices (that I don't approve of) and many mistakes without putting their safety at risk again. Besides, I can't pretend to understand an economy that rewards mukbangers, extreme eaters.*

While we celebrated, Jesse asked if they could look in the guest bedroom—not only had I hidden valuables on the day they moved in, they'd hidden valuables as well and thought they might have left something behind. I didn't ask what they'd thought to hide, but I did ask if I'd turned out to be the person they thought I was when we met.

"It's all about the shoes," Keyawna said.

"What?"

"You were wearing Comme de Garcons Converse—the ones with the red hearts and eyes. I told Jesse that anyone who knows to get those sneakers has to be cool."

The thing is, they'd been a birthday present. Had I known that they were cool, not to mention expensive, I never have would have picked them out. I'm not giving credence to magical thinking or the idea that the universe is working for any of us, but maybe she was just a little bit psychic?

---

* In 2019, *The New York Times* profiled a mukbanger whose YouTube channel, showing her feasting on seafood, brings in a million dollars a year.

Spirited Away

THERE ARE TIMES IN OUR lives when the story we tell ourselves about who we are no longer matches up to the story
we are actually living. At fifty-five, I wasn't sure who I was
anymore.

So many of the daily activities that defined my identity—my
life as a daughter, wife, and mother—had fallen away. Someone
meeting me just a short time earlier would have known me as a
caregiver for my aging parents. A regular in my mother's chair
exercise class, I'd even spearheaded the addition of KC and the
Sunshine Band's "Shake, Shake, Shake, Shake Your Booty" to
the instructor's all–Bing Crosby playlist. My ex and I had been so
joined at the hip that it seemed only appropriate to post this update
on Facebook: "After twenty years, *The Jeff and Annabelle Show* has
not been renewed. Thank you for all of your love and support over
the years. We hope you will continue to tune into our new solo proj-

ects."* I was a perennial room parent, leading the intrepid crew who'd chaperoned the fifth-grade camping trip. Parent volunteers were required to sign a contract pledging not to drink during the entire trip. You know when you really want a drink? When shepherding fifth graders into the wilderness for four days.

Pursuits both small and large seemed to take on outsized significance. I'd observed this in friends who were also carving out new identities or conducting wholesale reinventions in midlife. Alicia, who'd been an accountant with a spotty meditation practice, was now a prayer warrior leading womyn's workshops in the ancient Art of Circling, which as far as I could tell consisted of inviting girlfriends to download about their day while sitting in a circle. Another friend chucked her corporate consultancy because it no longer reflected "who I am in the world," which was better expressed by becoming a sudsy, fur-covered mobile pet groomer. A college classmate beat pancreatic cancer and hit the cancer-survivor speaking circuit, while a colleague who let her hair go gray was conscripted as a foot soldier in what *Glamour* magazine termed the "Silver Revolution." When my friend, ubermom, and hiking buddy Gia's third son applied for college, with one child left at home, she saw a future that didn't, as she put it, "rise to the level of chaos I function best in." She cooked up a plan to add six more years before her nest would empty. She and her husband adopted a daughter, and then deciding that "this boat can hold one more," they folded another

---

* Some friends were disappointed that our marriage was ending. "But what about your book about making a marriage work, *You Say Tomato, I Say Shut Up?*" I guess we ran out of tomatoes and had too much shut up was the best answer I could offer.

daughter into their brood. "I'll be almost seventy when they're all launched!" she told me with manic glee. Her plan misfired when the two older sons boomeranged back home and the first-year college student got "canceled on campus" and returned for a gap year. She wound up with six offspring under her roof and a perennially glazed look on her face.

I wasn't going to follow her lead, but motherhood had brought out the best in me. Not that anyone would characterize me as the warm and fuzzy maternal type, but after years of solipsistic career building, I endeavored to instill upstanding values and model good citizenship in my child. During grade school, Ezra and I had faithfully volunteered in the school's community soup kitchen and marched for peace.* It was the buildup of crappy plastic party favors in the back seat of my car that had sparked my environmentalism activism. I was that dinner party guest who could be found sorting through my hosts' trash to find that one stray potato peel or sliver of tinfoil to transfer to the compost pile or recycling bin. I carried soda-can-tab crocheted handbags stitched by Indigenous fair trade artisans and drove a hybrid. One fall I insisted on freecycling (a form of locally sourcing or scavenging pre-owned goods) our back-to-school supplies in lieu of shopping. Between raiding our neighbor's junk drawers next to the fridge and hitting up our local freecycling fellows, we ended up with enough crayons, markers, and construction paper to open our own arts and crafts store. Even though Ezra refuses to remember this teachable episode with anything other than an exasperated eye roll, I stand by this as one of my finest moments.

---

* At the first march we attended, Ezra and the other children's chant of "No More War" somehow morphed into "No More School." Still.

But without Ezra to model behavior for, I fell into bad habits. My mercurial recycling habit got iffy; what did I do when my La Croix pamplemousse sparkling water cans migrated into the regular garbage? I left them in there! Who was this depraved reprobate?

At the same time, I was facing down the annual Gurwitch Thanksgiving foodgasm. Navigating holiday travel and running the gauntlet of safe topics that can be broached with family members tests even the most sainted amongst us. Even more daunting can be living up to—or living down to, in my case—the role you play in your family's dynamic.

Despite whatever improvements motherhood had inspired, my place in the tribe as the unreliable, overly dramatic, if not beloved then at least be-liked family member was cemented decades ago. In my early twenties, I'd attended a cousin's wedding at a conservative synagogue in Houston wearing a pink polka-dotted strapless lamé minidress with a hoop skirt. On another occasion, I'd turned up with a surprise spouse, having just eloped. Later, as a harried working mother, I'd arrived late or canceled at the last minute. At one nephew's bar mitzvah I missed the religious ceremony entirely— granted, it was due to a work commitment, but my rental car ran out of gas, and I wound up hitchhiking to the reception. The story of my rescue from a dusty mountainside freeway exit ramp by another tardy guest is a family favorite.

Any glamour added by my minor public profile was subtracted by the oxygen I typically sucked out of the room, either by my own doing or as a feature of the annual Jeff and Annabelle Show Holiday Special. During our marriage, we took few vacations. Thanksgivings were an exception. We'd book a hotel, rent a car, and split our time between family obligations and leisure activities. You know what's an expectation that never pans out? That a family confab will double as a much-needed getaway. With our more liberal political stances, rejection of organized religion, and Stiller and Meara–inspired bickering, our presence ratcheted up tension around the dinner table.*

Providing an entertaining distraction was useful when my mother was alive. Loosening of internal filters has been linked to dementia, and it's possible that's what we were seeing, but we didn't realize it at the time. There were always relatives that she already wasn't speaking to, and every gathering was an opportunity to goad another unsuspecting reveler into not speaking to her. She had a talent for mentioning things that folks already knew, like inquiring if they'd gained weight. Had they put on a little weight? How much weight had they put on? How much weight did they think said cousin had put on? Once, she felt it necessary to inform me that my cat had gotten husky.

But the worst sin of all was that I'd always shown up without homemade provisions. At family meals, card games, coffee klatches, or any gathering of more than one person, my grandmother Rebecca rolled in with her legendary meatballs, stuffed cabbages, and enough banana bread to feed a small army. My nephew Max once brined a turkey and carried it on the plane, cradling it like an infant. Some people fly with their service animals; the Gurwitches travel with pies, kugel, and three-bean salads. My sister, the CEO of a

---

* When I called Anne Meara, a dear friend, to share the news that Jeff and I were planning on performing together like her and Jerry, Anne warned me of how hard it could be on a marriage. "Oh, my God, Annabelle, that's a terrible idea, don't do it!"

worldwide charity, regularly makes her own risotto—from scratch! Me? Everyone in the family knows that "I don't cook, I heat." I prefer to travel with a neck pillow.

This was going to be a banner year. I'd be both single and child-free—Ezra had elected to remain on campus. I would need to put a good face on it to avoid any questions about dating prospects and the touchy subject of Ezra's absence. Gurwitch family gatherings are considered sacrosanct, especially ones involving meals. It would also be the second Thanksgiving without my parents. As one of the oldest in attendance, I would be assuming the mantle of a family elder. Were any of my multitudinous character flaws befitting of my stature as a newly minted family elder?

Another landmark was that after decades of serving as party planner in chief, my sister was handing the reins over to her sons. This would be our first celebration at one of my nephews' homes. While my life had mutated into something unrecognizable, my nephews, Max and Brian, had come into their own. Both were working at well-established tech companies, and it was thrilling to hear about jobs that come with snack stations, campuses with bicycles, arcades, and nap pods. They'd both married highly accomplished women, one a doctor, the other a scientist—it was their world now, and that's the natural order of things.

There's a saying in the theater that there are no small roles, only small actors, but that's a load of crap. A supporting player can be distracting and throw a narrative off kilter. The same principle holds true of family dynamics.

A family elder should toss off bon mots with aplomb. She should offer sage advice, but only if asked. She should be of good cheer and throw in a well-placed joke if conversation lags. She should enter and exit gracefully, but without attracting undue attention. I would need to let go of my cherished role as scene-stealer because a family elder is the ultimate supporting player.

To add to challenges ahead, I'd thriftily opted to spend the night on the air mattress at Max's apartment. At a hotel, you can enjoy downtime from your beloved family by working your way through the minibar and soaking in your bathtub to your heart's delight, but an auntie sharing a bathroom with her nephew and his wife would need to be on her best behavior. If I were an oddsmaker, I'd bet big against my ability to pull this off.

Hoping a last-minute job might materialize that would prevent my attendance, I'd waited until three days out to book my ticket from Los Angeles to Oakland and scored a discounted seat on an off-brand airline on Kayak.com.

I was grumpier than usual on my way to the airport, nursing a sort of preemptive air-travel pissiness, anticipating more than the typical annoyances associated with flying. My flight was departing from a terminal I'd never been to, which might mean lengthy delays and unanticipated hoops to jump through. There was just one attendant behind the check-in desk when I arrived at what appeared to be a nondescript office building a few miles from the main airport. The attendant kept me waiting a mere ten minutes, but I allowed myself to sigh with more heft than I would have had Ezra been with me, certain I'd be hoofing it down corridors and boarding a shuttle bus to get to my gate. After checking me in, the attendant directed me to wait in the passenger lounge and pointed to a set of tinted glass doors.

I pushed open the doors and discovered that I wasn't in a terminal at all. I was in an airport hangar. Alone. Parked a few feet in front of me was a sleek white jet surrounded by red velvet ropes. It was polished to such shiny perfection it looked less like a form of transportation and more like an oversized toy. I was sure that my reservation, which had been advertised as a seat on an "empty leg," a return portion of a one-way private charter flight, was code for "you're traveling by crop duster or on a medevac and will be required to fly with an organ in a cooler on your lap." My ticket had cost less than $200. I'd never flown on a private plane, not only because I couldn't afford it, but having seen my fortunes rise and fall over the years, I'd championed a healthy suspicion of the trappings of wealth. I was a person of the people! Plus, private jet flights burn more greenhouse gases than the average American produces in a year. That stat is my typical scintillating dinner party small talk.

So I did what seemed to be the only appropriate thing in this situation: I took selfies with the jet, then texted friends, "This is my ride to Oakland!" "Holy shit!" I wrote, even though I never say that. In some kind of venal fugue state, I added another phrase I'd never used even once in my entire life, "Flying . . . *like a boss!*"

I took a seat in the passenger lounge, or rather, I stretched out across one of the half-dozen leather couches, separated from the jet by another row of red velvet ropes. My perch gave me an unobstructed front-row seat to take in the arrival of my fellow travelers. As they trickled in, I couldn't help but wonder who'd ponied up the airline's $50,000 annual membership fee and which of my fellow passengers were, like me, People of the Kayak.

A wisp of a woman floated in. She had on such a determinedly boxy and unflattering outfit it had to be made by some famous designer. She had three reed-thin, tousle-haired ragamuffins in tow. Having grown up in a middle-class family, I know that no mother

lets her children be seen looking like orphans in a community theater production of *Oliver Twist* unless they're loaded. Also, the children headed straight to a foosball table in the lounge area. You're a
kid and you don't have a holy-shit moment at seeing a jet a few feet
from you? I was positive the pockets were deep.

A squat, muscly sort in pressed jeans and a bomber jacket strode
in wearing a T-shirt advertising a company that made machine gun
parts. He was clutching the hand of a female companion in a way
that suggested she had been acquired to accessorize his outfit. His
fingers were pink and piggy. I hoped that if she was the hired help,
he was paying well, because I didn't like the way his swagger left
her trailing in his wake. I pegged them as paying full freight, but
when he released her from his grip, he not only shot selfies with the
jet, he recorded a video, giving a 360-degree turn as he narrated. I
downgraded them to Kayak.

A family of four entered the hangar, arms laden with Trader
Joe's bags. They had dressed with care: button-down shirts were
tucked in, khakis ironed, shoes shined. Before posing for pictures,
the mother licked the heel of her hand to paste down her child's hair
in a way that I recognized from my childhood. Kayakers.

The lounge was brimming with anticipation, silver trays were
overflowing with packaged baked goods, and there was an unmis-
takable collegial spirit. We were in this together, we few, we happy
few, we band of jet-setters. The free coffee was Nespresso, whose
plastic pods violated my single-use-item prohibition, but it seemed
impolite not to partake. I resisted the temptation to stuff the com-
plimentary snacks into my backpack, suddenly compelled to try to
pass as a frequent flyer—unlike bomber jacket dude, whose pockets
were bulging with biscotti.

When it was time for the dozen or so of us to board, we politely lined up alongside yet another set of red velvet ropes. (A lot of red velvets were sacrificed for our pleasure.) An attendant ushered us inside the aircraft with the care usually reserved for handling crystal champagne flutes. "No, you go ahead!" "No, you go ahead," we joked, treating our fellow travelers with commiserate magnanimous obeisance.

Sinking down into my plush leather padded stand-alone seat was like easing into a La-Z-Boy recliner. In 2019, *Forbes* published a study by a microbiologist showing 265 bacteria colonies on an airplane bathroom flush button, while 2,155 colonies were found on a tray table. Not this one. It was made of polished wood, blond with a swirling Mondrianesque grain, and squeaky-clean. I considered lopping it off and slipping it into my carry-on, like a serial killer's souvenir. I inhaled deeply: my seat smelled like leather and people who've paid off their college loans.

Flying time was less than two hours, which passed by so quickly and comfortably, I wondered if we'd bent the space-time continuum. I'd scarcely sunk into my flying Barcalounger and closed my eyes, and we'd already landed in Oakland.

I'd insisted to my kid that you can't buy happiness, but I'd been mistaken. I belonged here. This would be the new me: the Elegant Elder Gurwitch.

After deplaning, we were escorted to another private hub. This one had a working fireplace, board games for kids, warm chocolate chip cookies, and the truest signal that you're in an exclusive enclave: no line for the women's restroom. When my Uber whisked me away to the family gathering, I was feeling #blessed, #grateful, #instagrammable.

#Filledwiththemilkofhumankindness, I arrived uncharacteristically early and threw myself into a frenzy of usefulness: setting the table, tossing salads, and swooning over my nephew's dog Millie's intelligence and shiny coat despite my unwavering fealty to the feline species.* Thanksgiving dinner passed delightfully. Nothing irritated me, not the raised eyebrows over my failure to contribute a signature dish. "Silly family!" I trilled. "You know the only thing I cook up is trouble." Not the prospect of spending the night on an air mattress that looked as comfortable as a rack and pinion. "It looks positively cozy," I sang. Having been coddled like a poached egg, I could handle anything. Mentions of my inability to convince my offspring to attend? "Oh, family, it just means more white meat for us!" As I scoured the pots and pans, deftly deflecting queries about the state of my career and love life, I overheard a comment attesting to my new and improved attitude. Later, I took the briefest of showers so as to not tie up the single bathroom and to conserve hot water for my kindhearted hosts. The day had been claimed by the next generation, and I didn't even need to take my emergency Klonopin.

It was late that night, as I tossed and turned on my bed of nails, that I remembered I'd booked my return flight separately. I would be flying home on Spirit Airlines.

That next day, we the people, in order to form a more perfect TSA line, inched along, and a passenger knifed me in the back with their roller bag handle so that my six-dollar coffee dribbled down my torso, leaving a dingy brown stain on my white jeans. I was winded by the time I arrived at the gate, where there was one seat for every seven passengers. A family of five was sprawled out

---

* Millie the dog is, admittedly, affectionate and easy to love.

like human pick-up sticks. I was hangry but refused to fork over the money for a snack. (*Shoulda bagged that biscotti after all.*) When the boarding began, the crowd surged forward, jostling for position like jackals circling their prey. Just another face in the crowd, I was in group twenty-seven or forty-seven, I can't remember, but it didn't matter because I used the arthritis in my hands as an excuse to board with passengers requiring extra time. I thumped down on the deflated seat cushion with so much force that I wondered if I might bruise. I tested the seat-back tray table. What popped down was a metal sheet that looked like the kind of food tray you see in a correctional facility. I know this because I volunteered at the women's prison in Chino, because that's the kind of person I am! There was a balled-up tissue under my seat. I kicked it under the row in front of me.

I soon discovered that I would be traveling next to the Incredible Hulk. My seatmate was a furry beardo in gym shorts; at maybe six foot five, at least six feet of him seemed comprised of hairy leg. After takeoff, he put on his headphones and was instantly riveted by something on his phone, while my gaze was firmly fixed on his mastodon thigh. I was waiting for him to man-spread that meaty appendage and invade my space so that I could lay into him, but even though I shifted the tiniest bit toward him, he denied me the pleasure of incurring my ire. The two hours of flight time seemed to stretch into seven. I've never wrestled, but I imagine that being trapped in my seat must be what it's like to be pinned to the mat. I couldn't move a muscle.

Angling for a prime position to disembark, I edged my way past a grandma straining to dislodge her carry-on from an overhead compartment the size of a toaster oven. We streamed into the gate, the airport equivalent of Penn Station, and were hit with that signature scent of Los Angeles International Airport: a combination of Subway and stale coffee. The women's bathroom line snaked all the way into another Spirit Airlines boarding line and I had to wonder if this had ever caused any confusion of the "but this seat looked an awful lot like a commode" kind. I was rushing to the escalator leading to the baggage claim when I saw a mother struggling to open a stroller while balancing her infant child on her hip. I swooped in, folded and carried her stroller down the escalator for her, and then immediately cut in front of her so I could exit the terminal three seconds faster.

Wandering the parking structure, I punched the alarm button on my car remote key fob over and over, to no avail. Then it hit me. I had departed from Burbank, not Los Angeles, over an hour's drive away. I had booked my return flight to the wrong airport.

I jumped into a cab to avoid the crowded shuttle bus trip and long wait at the ride share waiting area, thereby erasing any savings I'd made by flying Spirit. On the cab ride to the private jet hub to retrieve my car, I closed my eyes and tried to pretend I was elsewhere. Was it only twenty-four hours earlier that I'd been swaddled in luxury?

Was I only able to be that Elegant Elder because I'd flown "*like a boss*"? Could I only summon my better angels when treated with kid gloves? No, I'm a person of the people! But kid gloves are so soft and smooth . . . I should get a pair this winter. No, kid gloves are made from baby goatskin! Baby goats that have been robbed of their lives and the chance to stand on my back in goat yoga! No, that's wrong too. I'm not the kind of person who wears baby animal skins, although I scarfed down our Thanksgiving turkey's remaining skin while standing over the sink under the guise of doing the dishes. But I did wash the dishes.

Hadn't I allowed Millie to lick my face, something everyone found adorable? Didn't that count as a ceding-the-spotlight personal growth triumph?* I'd also resisted telling my sister that she risked becoming a cliché of a mother-in-law by referring to Millie as her granddog. Wasn't that a demonstration of laudable restraint?

I'd redeemed myself with that stroller, hadn't I? A case could be made that having an awareness of how wasteful and polluting charter flights are, while still being willing to occupy an empty seat, risking moral and ethical turpitude, was a demonstration of a good citizenship. (OK, maybe that was a stretch.)

Was it possible that I'd never been that model citizen I'd congratulated myself on becoming? Had my child seen through this charade? Who was I kidding—we'd shared a Jack and Jill bathroom for eighteen years, so my weakness for expensive moisturizers must not have gone unnoticed.

As we chugged along, it occurred to me that this next chapter of my life was going to require a bigger imagination of myself than I'd anticipated. Perhaps Elegant Elder was a reach.

Then I had one of those blinding moments of clarity, or it might have been the onset of a migraine, or both. In the changing landscape of my life, the illusion of the self I'd carefully constructed was falling away, but there was one constant I could maintain. What's a

---

* I'm not a fan of dog licking. It's a prime example of encountering an "unexpected wet." Like when you grab onto a handrail on public transportation and it's damp. You don't know where that dog's tongue has been—or rather, you do know, you know all too well.

family gathering without a soupçon of delightful unpredictability? Every family needs an eccentric aunt.

We'd actually had one in our family. Aunt Beatrice died before I was born, but I'd heard about her exploits often during my childhood. As a young woman, Great-great-aunt Beatrice hoped to join the Bolsheviks, except that as she was a Jew, the revolution wasn't interested in her continued presence in Russia. She came to America and did piecework and union organizing in a garment factory in New York City. Families have long memories, and even decades later, relatives gossiped about how Bea brought her dirty underwear home for her mother to wash well into her thirties. Beatrice never married and retired to Los Angeles at a time when moving out West was scandalous for a woman alone, even a spinster aunt. Even more outrageous was that she embraced veganism and yoga before it was fashionable. My grandmother's eyes widened when she'd repeat, "That Aunt Bea, she ate nuts and berries and stood on her head all day." Beatrice was in her late eighties when she was struck and killed by a trolley car. I hoped to come to a better end, but I had a new role model.

So I did what seemed appropriate. I emailed my nephews to give them the pleasure of knowing that I'd done something reliably kooky and flown into the wrong airport. "I've outdone myself this time. Love you all, Auntie A." Aunt Bea set the bar high, but I could give her a run for the money. I'd stick to washing my panties myself, but whatever version of myself I was becoming, I was not going to own it, I was going to celebrate it.

They Got the Alias That We've Been Living Under

WE'VE COME A LONG WAY, baby. Hollywood has discovered midlife downward mobility. As Gloria Steinem told us, "If you can see it, you can be it," and although we might prefer to sail into our golden years on a yacht, there's satisfaction in being seen. Disgruntled empty nester whose kids have boomeranged and are sponging off you? Caregiving and plotting your exit strategy? Ghosted but refusing to be relegated to spinster purgatory? On screens big and little, the new old isn't putting her feet up by the fireplace with the man who fucked the funk out of her—she's burning down the house and toasting marshmallows over the charred embers. Our avatars are of an age to have presumably heard Debbie Harry's invitation to "die young and stay pretty," and to have thought better of it. There's a rousing quality to the onscreen depiction of women in midlife that's reminiscent of the 1969 Stonewall protests, when activists rallied the crowds with "We're here, we're queer, get used to it!" The less than subtle subtext of these films is "We're older, we're bolder, get used to it!"*

I grew up before Blockbuster, DVR, and streaming, when new movies ran for months at our local theater. Long after my memory goes—pets' names, kid's birthday, first-grade teacher, and the street I grew up on (my internet passwords)—all that will be left is the plot of the 1976 sci-fi thriller *Logan's Run*. I saw it at least a dozen times. Younger audiences will recognize the dystopian narrative in more recent films like *The Giver* and *The Hunger Games*. It goes like this: our planet can't sustain the population, so some of us must be sent "elsewhere." In *Logan's Run*, upon reaching the ripe old age of thirty, citizens must report for relocation to the utopian Sanctuary. Spoiler alert: when Logan "runs" to escape this fate, he and pals discover there is no Sanctuary; they are being harvested for food. Critics have long speculated that the film is a metaphor for the industry that gave us the faded, frightening spectacle of Gloria Swanson in *Sunset Boulevard*, but what I learned from *Logan's Run* was that thirty years old was a plausible expiration date.†

In the 1970s, thought-provoking films like *An Unmarried Woman*, starring Jill Clayburgh as an unconventional divorcée reinventing her life, were released, but I was too young for them to be on my radar, so my first peek at the midlife female in captivity was on the small screen. What's not to love about *The Golden Girls*, the sitcom in which three friends and one of their moms move in together to pool resources. They had their share of infighting, but what's a weekly

---

* I didn't come up with this slogan; it's the clever tagline of Next Tribe, a website and community for bolder women.
† Gloria Swanson was fifty when the film was shot.

show without conflict? The show is a bona fide cultural institution. How do we know that? *Golden Girls Live: A Musical Drag Parody* toured the country continuously for sixteen years, *RuPaul's Drag Race* did a tribute show to the Girls, and one of the most popular novena prayer candles you can purchase is the Saint Dorothy (Bea Arthur). The show was groundbreaking, tackling subjects like abortion and AIDS, and while the Girls weren't exactly put out to pasture, creator Susan Harris chose to set the show in South Florida, which at that time was commonly referred to as God's waiting room. Outfitted in dowdy pantsuits, shape-shifting sweater sets, and beauty-parlor bouffants, even the youngest of the Girls, Rue McClanahan (fifty-three), had a feathered 'do that was on the starched side. It's hard to reconcile these geriatric visuals when you consider that in the same year as the show premiered, 1985, Steinem, at fifty-one, just a few years shy of McClanahan, rocked a long loose bob and a figure-flattering ensemble at the premiere of *A Bunny's Tale*, based on her tenure at the Playboy Club.

A decade later, women of a definite age appear more contemporaneous in *How Stella Got Her Groove Back*, based on Terry McMillan's mega-bestselling book. Once lauded as a seminal midlife reinvention story, this film ushered in an era of fantastical yarns that followed a basic story line: A well-maintained woman in a well-appointed home wakes up in midlife to find that something is, well . . . missing. To overcome her doldrums, she is prescribed some kind of dramatic deliverance. In most cases, this cure takes the form of a man, an island vacation, or a dream house.

McMillan offers a seemingly modern theme: Stella has a high-powered job as a stockbroker, an impressive home, a killer wardrobe, and a successfully launched adult child. Alas, she longs for more. With all her privilege, hard earned as it is, it's tempting to yell that annoying twenty-first-century sentiment at the screen: "The something you're missing is gratitude!"

Stella is prescribed "the island cure" to reclaim her missing mojo. Travel is promoted, not so much for the purpose of immersion in another culture, but more as a mood stabilizer.

Stella jets to Jamaica, first class, of course, where she meets a Hottie McHandsome, twenty years her junior, who is immediately smitten. Just her luck, he's not a grifter; he's a Black Dr. McDreamy. It's gratifying to see a successful Black woman commanding the screen and inverting the standard male/female May/December love story, but it seems convenient that Stella is both wealthy and played by Angela Bassett, one of the most stunning women to have ever walked the earth. Arguably, Bassett is at peak goddess, which for her translates to any age she's ever been and ever will be.

If the film were titled *How Stanley Got His Groove Back*, our protagonist would have headed home with not so much as a "Thanks for the good time, sweetheart, now go buy yourself something pretty" tossed over his shoulder. Instead, Stella totes her island souvenir back to the mainland, and chucks her career to pursue a long-abandoned passion for woodworking. All she needs is love and, forgive me, some wood. When Stella is offered her high-flying gig back with a substantial raise *and* benefits and still turns the job down, I was once again tempted to yell, "Take the offer, lady, you have no idea what's coming!" Critic Roger Ebert wrote in his review, "I give them three weeks." What he said.

That same year, *Shirley Valentine* came out. Like Stella, Shirley of Liverpool takes a transformative island vacay. Shirley, cheekier and more down-market than Stella, is tired of waiting on her family members who want their tea freshened on demand and meals prepared to their exacting specifications. She flees to the Greek island of Mykonos, where she has a torrid affair, but this is where the film takes a much more realistic turn—the schmo is a serial seducer of tourists. Stalwart Shirley is undaunted. Having noticed that Brits traveling abroad prefer their own musty fare to fresh island catch, she opens a pub. It seems to me that Shirley has traded one set of problems for another. How soon before her customers' demands of "this kidney pie is cold" or "I ordered my bangers and ale ten minutes ago" start to sound just like her family's invectives?

Beginning in the 1980s, director Nancy Meyers assumed the mantle of she-who-would-make-the-world-safe-for-middle-aged-women by giving us center stage in her rom-coms. Only, in the majority of Nancy's comedies, the real stars are the houses that populate her stories. The inhabitants of these homes live lives of cushy desperation, untouched by the worries faced by most of us. An *Architectural Digest* feature described her interiors as creating the sensation of "being wrapped in a pillowy, line-fresh duvet or enveloped in cupcake batter." No film epitomizes this more than 2003's *Something's Gotta Give*.

The movie is about a gracious Cape Cod beachfront cottage. With toasty shingles on the outside and warm, fluffy vanilla interiors, it's less dwelling than live-in baguette. The wooden floors are as shiny as a glazed ham, while the paint on the walls looks so rich it might be fondant. Each of the shabby-chic cream-colored couches, draped with camel and caramel throws, is deliciously overstuffed, probably with hundred-dollar bills.

Oh, and people come in and out of the house and do stuff. Diane Keaton is always winning, and here she wafts in and out of her world without shadows, in clothes so crisp that they appear to have never been touched by human hands. Her hair has the kind of honeyed highlights that must be tended to so frequently that one suspects there's a hair salon and stylist stationed 24/7 in one of her many bedrooms.

Keaton is a fabulously successful playwright who spends lonely nights nestled in casual opulence, until she unexpectedly finds herself with not one but two suitors: Keanu Reeves, another selfless dreamboaty doctor, and the affable but loutish Jack Nicholson. You just know that Nicholson, something of an overstuffed couch himself, is going to win out because Keanu is a sleek Eames and he's never going to match her décor.

Meyers is a masterful storyteller, and when I was younger, my bank account more padded, and I had more earning years ahead of me, I assumed Meyers was showing us what we could expect our future lives to look like. I enjoyed the "house porn" oeuvre, even though the film leaves an essential question unanswered: Will the couple make their main domicile Keaton's beachfront manse or Nicholson's elegant Upper East Side brownstone? With nary a whiff of financial worry, watching this movie is like rubbernecking the social conventions of an alternate universe.

Another Diane was pressed into service as our Everywoman in the trenches, in not one but four outings. Diane Lane was sent to battle back midlife malaise on our behalf, a testament not only to her strength as an actress but to her reassuring presence onscreen. Contrast Lane with Jennifer Jason Leigh, another terrific actress just three years her senior. With her sly squint and erratic energy, when Leigh makes an entrance, you instantly know—here comes trouble. Lane's even-keeled durability is comforting, making her the khaki pant of middle-aged actresses.

In the 1999 *A Walk on the Moon*, set in 1969, Lane plays a woefully unappreciated Jewish housewife. Does this inspire her to pursue a meaningful career or devote herself to charitable causes? Nope. She opts for the man cure and has an affair with a traveling (blouse) salesman who services the Catskill camp where she summers with her family. Viggo Mortensen is the "blouse man" who sells from the back of his converted school bus. Viggo Mortensen? In what world do unhappy Jewish suburbanites luck into liaisons with Aragon, Ranger of the North? After I let folks know that my husband and I were splitting, one of my neighbors, the "ice cream man" who distributes a line of ice cream to several local groceries, informed me that he frequented nude beaches, and if I had some girlfriends, we could all pile into his old truck and go together. Paunchy, hair spouting from all the wrong places, Ranger of Nada.

In *Unfaithful*, Lane's 2002 tour of duty, she conducts an unexpected (and unmotivated) affair with French actor Olivier Martinez, who is drop-dead gorgeous. Overly contrived meetings in films have been codified as "they meet cute," but in this case, "they meet clichéd." Laden with shopping bags, Lane loses her balance on a cobblestone street in Manhattan and topples into Martinez, an antiques dealer, who is himself burdened with a stack of leather-bound books. Volumes of romantic poetry.

This hunky foreign lover is killed by Lane's husband, played by Richard Gere. The scenes play out in the couple's suburban manse, Martinez's stylish Soho loft, and Gere's Mercedes E320. The title could have been *When Bad Things Happen to Beautiful People in Spectacular Settings*.

Lane headlines 2003's *Under the Tuscan Sun*, one of those "every-thing gets tied up in a bow" female fantasy fulfillment films that is chock full of the genre's familiar tropes (and based on another mon-ster bestseller). In *Sun*, Lane's friends pack her off to Tuscany. If she seems a tad on the milquetoast side, never fear—she's blessed with quirky best friend Sandra Oh, just like Bassett's Stella had a saucy sibling played by always-saucy sister Whoopi Goldberg.*

An update to the familiar plotline of sending a gal for the travel cure is that they they're sending her on a gay tour. She still man-ages to fall in love! With a house! *Che bello!* She makes an offer on a villa and buys it on the spot. I happened upon this film as I was scrambling to refinance my home. When Lane got a home loan ap-proved in under five minutes, with no visible source of income, I was tempted to throw my Staples Easy Button at my TV, but I couldn't afford to replace the screen. The place isn't a Meyersian palace that she can ease into like a cozy bedroom slipper; it's a fixer-upper, which makes for madcap scenes of home improvement humor. Con-venient plot twists ensue. The villa has its own vineyard! The vine-yard has but one sad, shriveled, dried-up grape, but vineyards can be resuscitated, just like women's vaginas! And in Female Fantasy Filmlandia, the most handsome men are stationed on every street corner just for the plucking! Unlike any of my exes, these dream-boats always seem to be licensed EMTs in vaginal resuscitation. But wait, there's more! In the end, we learn that during the renovation, Lane's character was writing the bestseller the movie was based on,

---

* Lane doesn't have a neurotic bone in her body, but if my friends could have af-forded to send me to Italy after splitting with my husband, I suspect they would have gotten a one-way ticket because they needed a break from my complaining.

proving that even though experts routinely tell us that its time has come and gone, never bet against khaki.

Lane also serves up a series of feasts in the film, and not only does each lavish spread look more expensive than the last, I have to wonder: when does slaving over a stove in Tuscany became just like slaving over a stove in the United States? A stove is a stove is a stove. I think it's a particular form of punishment to have a plotline that involves midlife and cooking—I mean, particularly if you're a mother, how many hours have you already logged in a kitchen?

Yet, of all the leaps of faith this film requires, there is one that I simply cannot wrap my head around. Where is the scene where she realizes that the contractor has taken a shortcut and piggybacked the plumbing from the upstairs to the downstairs, which means the water pressure will never be more than a trickle in her master bathroom, or the blow-up when she learns that the renovation will cost twenty thousand more than the estimate, or that inevitable day when the work crew simply stops showing up? The renovation comes off without a hitch, the results are resplendent, and she throws a wedding for one of her workmen. Somewhere in the world, contractors watch this film together and laugh their heads off.

In 2008, Lane is prescribed the island cure once more in *Nights in Rodanthe*, based on yet another bestseller. *Nights* could be summed up as a film about what happens when someone with great hair and teeth meets someone else with great hair and teeth.

Beset with marital problems, Lane's BFF, who happens to own the most picturesque romantic inn perched on the most picturesque beach on the picturesque island just off the coast of picturesque North Carolina, offers her a lifeline. Wouldn't you know it, her friend needs her to fill in as innkeeper on a weekend when a storm front and the handsomest boomer alive are both expected to arrive. Richard Gere is going to be the only guest at the inn. Paired with Lane again, this time Gere is a rich doctor who has also killed someone, but it was during a surgery, and he is very, very, very contrite, hence lovable. Lane is tasked to turn down his bed and cook and serve him his dinner as well.* This may be the only realistic part of the film: man falls for a female caretaker/nurse/server/private dancer.

There's tossed seas, tossed salad, and a good tossing between the sheets. They have the kind of dreamy movie sex that dissolves time from that first kiss until their postcoital embrace. No one ever worries about the wet spot in these montages, making them exactly unlike any sex any person on earth has ever had. Sadly, Dr. Gere brings bad weather wherever he goes, and soon after their weekend together, he dies in a mudslide while caring for underserved villagers in some remote region of the planet, before the couple ever has a chance to burp or fart in front of each other. The ending, which sees Lane smiling on a pier, suggests that one weekend with Gere was enough to revive Lane for the rest of her life. *American Gigolo*, indeed.

After *Nights* came out, throngs of women flocked to the Inn at Rodanthe. Entire industries sprung up to satisfy those wanting to take cooking classes in Tuscany and experience *Shirley Valentine*–themed Greek excursions. There is no end to the blogs, books, and

---

* Cooking is regularly employed as a way of endearing a female character to audiences. Even in *Something's Gotta Give*, Keaton, a successful playwright, must demonstrate her womanly skills in the kitchen. Cooking says, "I am a nurturer, not some raging hormonal harridan."

Instagram accounts detailing the attempts of women and a few intrepid men to mirror the transformative experience of *Eat, Pray, Love*, the juggernaut of the travel cure films (and books). My favorite is the Instagram account of @vettravellove. She describes her adventures as being "like *Eat, Pray, Love* but with more spaying." I also have a special appreciation for the travel cure backlash bloggers like Julia Hamilton, who offers sound advice to seekers on a budget at shutupandgo.travel. Instead of trekking across the globe, Hamilton suggests that an equal amount of profundity can be accomplished through taking a meditation class and calling our mothers.

In my own circle, three close friends, a few years my senior, tested out the island cure after seeing *Shirley Valentine*.

One visited Whidbey Island, north of Seattle across Puget Sound, where she fell in love and married, not a Dr. McDreamy, but a nice dentist with kind eyes.

Another friend, a divorcée, Trini was sure that island life would lead to sexual escapades and she'd finally write that novel, something she'd never found the time to do during her marriage and years of raising children. She moved to an island off the coast of Massachusetts where her family summered, but she hadn't anticipated the high cost of year-round living, limited employment opportunities, and an even smaller dating pool. The men she met were also reinventing on a budget: they had Ivy League degrees and were working as carpenters. Trini got her wild affair and a set of built-in bookcases, but soon enough, island fever set in. She took a vow of chastity and gave up bras, which she found "freeing" if somewhat distracting to others, but more worrisome was that five years in, she got rid of her car and was camping out in a garage apartment without running water. Friends, myself included, worried for her welfare, convinced her to move back on the mainland. She's living in the guest room of one of her adult children. The novel didn't pan out, but you knew that already.

Another friend, Joann, is faring better in her chosen island home, teaching school part time and enjoying a lively social life, although the apocryphal island romance did not materialize. Set up with someone described as "a real character" (always a red flag), she attended a BBQ at his house during which he alternately insisted that they'd dated earlier in life (they hadn't) and that she'd once side-swiped his car in the parking lot of the local market (she's certain she would have remembered that). Then, while grilling kebabs, his pants fell down and he left them there until the meat was cooked. The kicker is that he has three erudite sisters whose company she enjoys, so she continues to attend his gatherings and he routinely insists that they once collided, but that's the price of female companionship on an island.

I've never taken the island cure, but I once taught a workshop at the Canyon Ranch and got more than a little excited when a cute guy asked for my phone number. It turned out he wanted to sell me Nerium skin care products and talk me into joining his downline.

Here's the good news: for those of us experiencing shortfalls, financial, emotional, or otherwise, the offerings are plentiful. There's Netflix's *Otherhood*, where a trifecta of badass mothers from the 'burbs contrive the perfect revenge for phone calls their adult sons have sent straight to voicemail: showing up unannounced for extended visits. The film got over 21 million viewings, making it one of Netflix's most popular films of 2019.

If your kid has ever said, "Mom, you're so embarrassing," you'll relish the tense standoffs between a geekily repressed son and his free-spirited sex educator mom Gillian Anderson in *Sex Education*. Annette Bening does double duty as Our Lady of Single Motherhood and Boarding House Den Mother of the Year in *20th Century Women*. Empathetic and intelligent, Bening's standout performance reminds us that class doesn't come with a price tag.*

If mid-century motherhood had its own awards show, Most Beleaguered Working-Class Mom would go to Laurie Metcalf in *Lady Bird*. Saoirse Ronan is affecting as a young woman coming of age in Greta Gerwig's 2017 film, but long-suffering, deadpan mama Metcalf, described as "scary but warm" by one of her daughter's friends, steals every scene. She's overworked at her hospital job, her unemployed husband passes his days playing cards online, and her boomeranger son and his girlfriend have taken up residence on the fold-out living room couch. On top of that, Metcalf's daughter, a high school senior, to whom she gave the perfectly serviceable name of Christine, insists on being addressed as Lady Bird, and that's the least of her entitled and self-absorbed personality traits. Also, the entire family shares one bathroom.

My only unrequited wish is to redo the scene in which Lady Bird, a newly minted college student, phones her mother to say that she's all right after a night of heavy drinking. In my version, Lady Bird reaches a recording letting her know that her mother's phone number is no longer in service. Metcalf's hubby has hit the jackpot in an online poker game! The camera finds them living it up at a

---

* I am not including *Schitt's Creek* here, only because the series tells the story of an entire family's adventures in downward mobility. Catherine O'Hara's performance is miraculous and she should be canonized as the patron saint of the downwardly mobile.

wine tasting in Napa. Mama Metcalf is wearing a T-shirt that reads
KEEP CALM AND MAKE IT YOURSELF.

The Oscar for Best Low-Rent Reinvention would go to
Juanita. The film has been described as a Black, working-class
version of *Eat, Pray, Love*, but that doesn't do its offbeat, quirky
charm justice. The stakes are far higher for Juanita, played by
Alfre Woodard, to ditch her life than for Julia Roberts in *E, P,
L*. Juanita is saddled with a soul-crushing job, two boomerang-
ers, and a grandchild rooming with her when she steps away to
save her sanity. Juanita is also saddled with what are sometimes
unkindly referred to as saddlebags. Woodard, with her expressive features and luminous skin, is an original beauty, and with
hips that sway more than, say, Lane's sculpted physique, she is
recognizable as someone whose days don't include a BootyBarre
workout. Whew.

Juanita Greyhounds it to Butte, Montana, a town she picks
at random and mistakenly refers to as "Butt." She falls in love or
lust or something, but that's secondary to taking over the town's
woefully dysfunctional diner. The locals really seem to need a
"Black woman cooking," as she puts it. It is still a film where a
woman spends time in the kitchen, but it's quirky and the cast-
ing so inspired, it's forgivable here. Juanita's recurring sex fantasy is to have Blair Underwood: have him massage her aching
feet, that is. There's nothing Pollyanna about it—her lover lives
in a trailer with an outdoor fridge. Getting to see minimum-wage
middle-aged folks eating, praying, and loving seems even more
timely than the filmmakers might have imagined when it went
into production in 2017.

If there were a lifetime achievement award, it should go to

director and writer Nicole Holofcener, who has been chronicling the lives of ordinary women since her 1996 *Walking and Talking*, in which two friends negotiate the ups and downs of the friendship through a lot of . . . walking and talking. Her 2010 film *Please Give* was a nuanced exploration of the limitations of do-gooderism that provided no feel-good conclusion. Her screenplay for 2018's *Can You Ever Forgive Me?* tells writer Lee Israel's true story and manages both sympathy and revulsion for the former bestselling author who turned to literary forgery when she fell on hard times. It should be required viewing for English majors.

In 2006's *Friends with Money*, Jennifer Aniston plays a woman whose friends' fortunes have risen while she ekes out a living cleaning houses. Aniston is shown hoofing it from store to store to yet another store to collect as many pricey product samples as she can hustle up. When she couldn't resist raiding her client's stash of that very same budget-busting moisturizer and slathering her feet with it, I was cheering her on.*

But it was her *Enough Said* (2013) that made me wonder if Holofcener had placed a listening device in my home. Her protagonist, a more vulnerable Julia Louis-Dreyfus than we typically see onscreen, undergoes no major life reinvention. Instead, she weathers the minor tragedies of the middle-aged. A massage therapist who makes house calls, she's lugging her table up and down steep staircases, her couch is saggy, and her spirits are flagging when she and James Gandolfini meet. Their hookup is a comedy of errors: his arm

---

* When I interviewed Holofcener in a *New York Times* piece about my own obsession with samples, Holofcener confessed that she, like me, worries about future penury and pocketed all the samples used in that scene.

is trapped under her hair and their bodies don't exactly fit together, and they laugh a lot. It's utterly charming and recognizable to anyone who has started dating after a long hiatus and discovered that it's not, as the aphorism goes, "just like riding a bike." In my experience, it's more like you used to ride a ten-speed whose gears you mastered and now you've got to learn to ride a Fixie. Also priceless is a plotline in which Louis-Dreyfus, anticipating her empty nest, attempts to poach her daughter's best pal, as well as when she makes a disastrous misjudgment in a desperate bid for female companionship. As if all that weren't enough, Holofcener gives us a lovable, if flawed, woman who cooks for no one.

A special citation would be granted to Chilean director and writer Sebastián Lelio for gifting us with not one but two glorious *Gloria*s. Both his 2013 Spanish-language original starring Pauline Garcia and his 2019 American *Gloria Bell* starring Julianne Moore are lightning in a bottle. In both films, Gloria is a divorcée who spends her days at a straitlaced office job and her nights on the dance floor. Neither Gloria is particularly well heeled, but both are poised and put together. Money is tighter in Chile, so Santiago Gloria waxes her own legs, while her Los Angeles counterpart frequents a salon. Angeleno Gloria has an office with a door, while in Santiago Gloria is trapped in a cramped cubicle, but both toil in equally thankless positions as insurance claim adjusters. Lelio wants us to know that Gloria is empathetic to the economic unrest in the world around her, so Garcia is swept into a street protest and Moore acts as sounding board to an officemate with less job security. Moore shouts "Appreciate this woman!" into the parking structure where she and her coworker take a smoke break. Needless to say, no one is listening.* The revelation of the American film is that despite Julianne Moore's rarefied, almost alien elegance, she is convincingly ordinary. The word "mousy" comes to mind.

Lelio and the actresses pull off close magic as we watch Gloria negotiate the daily indignities of life lived as an Everywoman. Like Diane Keaton in *Something's Gotta Give*, Gloria takes a chance on love, gets her heart broken, and must summon the strength to put the pieces back together. Keaton takes long luxurious walks on her private beach and even longer walks from her bedroom to her kitchen, a distance that appears almost as lengthy as the coastline. Keaton must settle for the acclaim of her hit Broadway show, redecorating her Manhattan pied-à-terre, and the adoring arms of Keanu Reeves—nobody's idea of a consolation prize—before ultimately getting her man. On the other hand, Gloria's age and status act as cloaks of invisibility as she travels the world, drawing little attention. Gloria throws herself into a *liaison dangereuse* after being unceremoniously dumped by her caddish paramour while on a beach holiday. Her pitiable midlife morning-after "walk of shame" on a public beach is nothing at all like Keaton's restorative strolls.

With "Total Eclipse of the Heart" blasting from the speakers of her Toyota compact, Gloria girds herself for vengeance with a carpool karaoke that will never land her in the passenger seat of James Corden's car. Armed with gumption and a paint gun, she sprays the side of the creep's house, an action both toothless and triumphant.

---

* The lot where they're commiserating looks an awful lot like the Santa Monica parking structure where in real life several middle-aged writers, overcome with anxiety over flailing careers, jumped to their deaths in 2019.

Could it be that Gloria is also giving the finger to all of those midlife movie "cures"?

The next time we see Gloria, she is sitting alone at a wedding reception when Laura Branigan's "Gloria" comes on. A would-be suitor asks her to dance and she sloughs off his entreaty, like she's exfoliating him. Instead, she strides toward the dance floor. Alone in a crowd of revelers, she stands completely still and we wonder: Is this when Gloria crumbles? Eyes closed, one arm raised, her fist pulses, beating out a rhythm, like a heartbeat. In that instant, a light switch is flipped on from inside and we see Gloria's inner radiance, and in a transcendent unedited sequence, Gloria turns into Julianne Moore, beaming at maximum movie-star wattage. It's movie magic in real time. Our Everywoman has been transformed, not by a new career, new man, new house, or new handbag, but through self-possession. With a slight tilt of her head, Gloria snaps her fingers, and she is the dancing queen.

We don't know what's next for Gloria, but as Branigan sings, it seems clear that Lelio wants us to know that "the alias that [she's] been living under," to quote the lyrics of the song, was a lesser version of herself, one that she has exorcised and torched.

Something about the way Gloria snapped her fingers jogged another memory from my childhood. In *Bewitched*, Samantha's finger snap transported her to anywhere she needed to go. But my favorite character in *Bewitched* was always Endora, Samantha's mother, played by Agnes Moorehead, who swanned around the house in outfits worthy of Iris Apfel. As a young person, I knew Endora was intended as comic relief. Now, I think she got the last laugh. Her spells were stronger than her daughter's, because as everyone knows, a witch's power grows with age. Huh. Endora might be our best role model of all.

Lubepocalypse Now!

"ARE YOU SEEING ANYONE YET?"

After concerns over where I'd be residing, this was invariably the next question that friends, family, and even casual acquaintances asked after my husband and I parted ways. When I said I wasn't interested in dating, people reacted as if I'd broken the social contract. My friend Carla, recently widowed and actively searching for a new partner, was apoplectic.

"But it's just what we do. Everyone needs someone to have dinner with, like salt and pepper shakers," Carla said. I wasn't sure if I wanted to share dinner with someone, much less find what has been euphemistically called a "toe-tag" partner, a companion to see you through until, well, toe-tag time.

The assumption was that I was careening toward only two plausible futures: shut-in or cat lady. This absorption over whether or not I was seeing anyone seemed confirmation of not only my waning capacity as a wage earner, but my minor accomplishments in the world at large. I have a hard time imagining people asking Jane Goodall, "So, are ya seeing anyone, Janie?"

Every single person in my life offered advice. Erika insisted that we meet for drinks, so she could share her field research on dating. We convened at a local watering hole where she ordered a cheese board garnished with dried figs. She delicately fingered two pieces of fruit and presented them in her palm.

"Are you fond of these?"

"Yes?" I answered tentatively, wondering where this was going.

"Good, because unless you want to *cougar* it, it's all saggy nut sack from here on in."

I confessed to having had a fleeting crush on a septuagenarian, a brilliant scholar. We'd attended an event in his honor together. As we forked our baby lettuces, I noticed his tongue rooting around his mouth in an attempt to dislodge food stuck between his teeth. The effort didn't produce that sucking sound associated with the elderly diner, but I couldn't shake the image of wiping crumbs from his chin after his next stroke (he'd had one recently). I dismissed the idea of becoming his lover/nursemaid somewhere between the rubber chicken and the baked Alaska.

"You know what you should do? Find some random dick."

I understood that she wasn't suggesting I find myself an asshole, but I've never been a casual hookup gal.

"Every penis comes attached to a person, and every person has a story, and I don't want to hear anyone's story," I told her. I also didn't want to tell anyone my story.

Erika shrugged. "When you're ready." She popped two especially wrinkly figs into her mouth and added, "And with a little blue pill, they're ready."

Online daters were gung-ho that I give it a shot. Like dieters who've adopted extreme regimens, juice cleanses, or intermittent fasting, they insist that you have to try it too, because it provides confirmation that it works.

The thing is, online does work. My friend Lara met her French scientist husband, with whom she has two gorgeous and whip-smart daughters, on Tinder. My neighbor John found his partner on SilverDaddies.com. Even Christine, a conservative Christian, who matched on Match with her stepbrother and a dude who went by the name Bling Bling, insisted I give it a shot. The iconic author Anne Lamott is betrothed to a man whom she met on the Our Time dating site.*

My sister, having also met her partner online, insisted I follow her lead. I suspect she was motivated by the fear that if I weren't successfully re-paired, I would become her problem in the future. She'd taken note of my chronic neck pain, assumed there was more of that to come, and imagined herself changing my light bulbs, driving me to physical therapy, and shopping for my groceries.

I explained that I was trying to put some emotional distance between my twenty-two-year marriage and whatever came next, but after six months, my friends and family weren't having it. "I'm practicing 'radical aloneness,'" I told them. As any grammarian will remind you, there's no need to qualify the word "alone" with "radical," just like there's no need to characterize anything as "to-

---

* So many of the newly divorced feel they've become experts through their hard-won experience that in 2019, *The New York Times* featured a story about the dating advice services Style My Profile and the Divorce Minder, both founded by middle-aged divorcées.

tally empty." Either something is empty or it is not. But in Los Angeles, the word "radical" carries unimpeachable heft. At any given
moment, locals are practicing "radical empathy" or "radical hon-
esty." As I write this sentence, someone in my zip code is leading a
workshop on "radical Swiffering."

It was concerning that since the split and with my kid out of the
house, time spent thinking about, talking about, sending cute photos and videos of, and cuddling and conversing with my cat were
occupying a disproportionate number of my waking hours. Then I
coaxed the cat, who had snoozed at the foot of our marital bed, into
sleeping on my feet. Over time, he'd migrated onto my chest. It took
six months until he stopped resisting my training him to sleep, head
wedged under my chin, body draped across my rib cage. I'd lower
my jaw like a panini press and fall asleep, face buried in his fur.
After a luncheon where I over-shared this information, an adorable
bubbie grasped my wrist, pulled me close, and whispered, "Sweetheart, if you ever expect to get laid again, you need to lose the cat."
When nonagenarians weigh in on your sex life, you probably should
listen, but I had practical reasons to eschew dating.

Getting a restful night of sleep means the difference between my
generalized dyspepsia and being specifically annoyed with every
person who crosses my path. I must have a firm wedge between my
knees, a smooshy cushion to lean into, a sturdy bolster supporting
my spine, and a sloped Tempur-Pedic travel pillow angled under
my neck. Also, I prefer to be cocooned in a heavy down comforter
or two. I am partial to sleeping in socks, a knitted hat, a scarf (if the
room is drafty), and a night guard to prevent TMJ clenching. The
only thing missing from this sexy picture is a sleep apnea machine,
and my GP just informed me that I might be headed toward one.

The pièce de résistance is my sleepwear: a microfiber bathrobe. The fabric is so silky that I suspect it is woven out of angel's breath and butterfly wings, but its bulkiness makes it the first cousin of a Slanket. Sold on late-night TV in commercials depicting American families lounging like beached whales while watching late-night TV, the "blanket with sleeves" gives one the appearance of wearing an adult onesie. My bathrobe makes the Slanket seem sexy. I've banned candles from my house because if this franken-fabric gets anywhere near an open flame, I'll be toast. And if I should self-immolate, friends and family will chalk it up to my refusal to date.

Still, these are merely transactional problems. There were emotional justifications for my lack of interest in partnering with anyone. Since the death of my parents, it occurred to me that any person I might be with in the future would never meet them. I loved my parents, in spite of their quirky fallibilities. My mother could always be counted on to ask "Can I interest you in a cheap Merlot?" at any time of day, and Dad always had a disarmingly inappropriate question at the ready: "Are you on the menu?" He delighted in tormenting waitresses. I would be denied the satisfaction of gesturing in their direction and then back at myself and saying, "See, this is why!"

After a starter marriage and my floundering divorce, *maybe*, I thought, *I'm just not good at relationships.** But I reconsidered my dating moratorium after reading about the Great American Sex Drought.

---

* There has been a rise in divorce for people over fifty, what's being termed "gray divorce." My spouse and I were into our third year of separation without officially divorcing, due to health insurance and tax advantages, giving new meaning to the term "gray divorce."

According to the data, in 2019, the number of Americans not having sex had increased to 50 percent. Pushing up this percentage is the number of aging Americans, sixty years old and older. Because this group is growing relative to everyone else, it has the net effect of statistically reducing the overall population's likelihood of having sex. Though not yet sixty, I could see the future.

During a drive to a concert, my friend Robyn, mother of three, twice divorced, an accomplished professional, and drop-dead gorgeous, confided that the last time she'd had sex, five years prior, it was unsatisfying on every level. With each block we drove, more details emerged: his poor technique, her lack of attention span for intimacy. By the time we got to the venue, she'd revised her estimation. It had been eight years since she'd had sex. After she parallel parked, she was up to nine and content with never having sex again.* The handwriting was on the wall. I imagined sending out notices to old lovers:

> *Dear paramours from days gone by,*
> *I'm closing up shop. Thank you for your patronage and, with only a handful*
> *of exceptions, a satisfying run of genuine orgasms.*
> *Internally yours, Annabelle*

Wasn't it something of a civic duty to help Make America Wet Again? I cautiously put out the word that I was open to dating.

But whom would someone be getting to know on a date with me?

---

* Jane Fonda recently announced, "I'm eighty. I've closed up shop down there." I appreciate and support that decision; I just wasn't sure I was ready to do the same.

On one early attempt at dating, I'd turned up for dinner and my date gasped, "What are you wearing on your feet?"

"I call them my hooves," I said, Vanna Whiting a pair of forest-green leather booties. Reactions to them typically range from "adorably elfin" to "you look like a centaur."

The next thing I knew, he was flooding my email in-box with screenshots of towering stilettoes. "You could really rock these."

"I'm not the kind of woman who dresses to please men," I replied. "Pumps are the footwear of the patriarchy!"

"Are you always this opinionated?" he asked.

"Oh, there's more where that came from!" What now? Was I becoming someone with a *catchphrase*? I'd heard that people become more set in their ways as they age, and I appeared to be morphing into a funhouse mirror version of myself: a crotchety old broad adopting strident positions on the sociopolitical messaging of heels.

When I relayed this episode to my sister, Lisa said, "You're overthinking this. Just be you," adding, "but be a version of yourself that's not so anxious." Was there such a version?

Less than twenty-four hours later, an email landed in my in-box alerting me that my sister, who had witnessed the erection-killing bathrobe, had signed me up for a subscription service called Lingerie Box. It's like Birchbox, only it wasn't beauty products but undergarments that would arrive at my doorstep. The email invited me to describe my taste in lingerie so that my box could be tailored especially to my liking. There was zero awareness of the double entendre in the email. A survey asked what I preferred: *flirty, sexy, something else?* I had no idea if they meant *flirty* in a Suicide Girl way—like ripped fishnets—or *flirty* like a 1950s pinup. I entered *spinstery*, but it wasn't a choice the algorithm recognized. I entered

Miss Havisham, but as that wasn't a valid choice either, I headed to the website to check out their wares.

To my relief, the site didn't feature your typical glammed-up models, crawling on all fours, looking famished, like undernourished big cats. The models were realistically curvy. My favorite was a matronly redhead with generous hips who looked like a grown-up version of your cousin Rosalie, the "bad girl" your parents warned you to stay away from because she ditched school, wore short shorts, and was caught making out under the bleacher stands. Rosalie had crepey, lined skin, like she was once a heavy smoker, and her décolletage had age spots. She was top-heavy, but not in a surgically enhanced way, and she had underarm cleavage, back fat, and negative stomach toning. I thought I spotted stray pubic hairs peeking out from her high-waisted panties; alas, I was disappointed to realize that my computer screen was just dirty.

I requested Rosalie's ensemble, but what arrived seemed to be a Girl Scout crafting project: a bralette fashioned out of bandage gauze glued to elastic strips. The matching polyester panties didn't have a cotton crotch. Still, it was an improvement over the bathrobe.

Not only were panties showing up on my doorstep at an alarming rate, but friends like Emily, one of the writers with whom I share office space, were offering unsolicited tips. "You've got to get Pjur lube, it's the best. It saved my life when I dated a drummer with an enormous cock." Since then, I've been unable to look at Emily without picturing an overly endowed rocker tracing her areolae with drumsticks while entering her from behind.

My friend Meredith weighed in. "Honey, do you really want to go through life never having been eaten by a woman? We know better than anyone what to do." I'd told her about a dinner party where I flirted with a rakishly handsome writer only to realize days later that it was the legendary queer punk poet Eileen Myles.

If I were to switch teams at this stage in the game, I wouldn't be the first. Even in the late nineteenth century, it wasn't uncommon for women to make this late-in-life switch and shack up together. Back then, it was referred to as a "Boston marriage."

"The thing is," I said to Meredith, "I'm happiest in the company of women, but I'm not sure I could 'do unto others as I would have them do unto me,' which is the one rule in life I try to live by."

While I paused, mulling over what seemed like an offer, Meredith qualified herself. "It's so good, especially if it's very *clean* down there," she said in such a pointed way that I suspected I would never be tidy enough for her. Two hours later she sent me a video.

"Hi Annabelle, I'm Meredith's gynecologist, Doctor Name Redacted." The doctor held up a collection of pink dildos, graded from average to jumbo-sized and packaged like hot dogs. "If you're planning to have sex after not having it for a long time, you'll need a set of these, come and see me."

What kind of doctor makes a video like that for someone she's never met? I couldn't read the medical degrees hanging on the wall behind her, but I hoped for Meredith's sake that she hadn't graduated from the University of Phoenix online.

My friend Jill insisted I come over immediately to brainstorm my return to houghmagandy, as the kids called it in the 1700s. "I'm worried that my middle-aged sex face might look too much like my I've-sprained-my-ankle face." She invited me to try it out on her. Eyebrows raised, lips parted, head tilted back, light panting. I was sure it looked like a desperate plea for hydration. "You're fine, besides, men don't even look at the face," she said, adding that she rarely thought about having sex with her husband of fifteen years, but that she was happy he still initiated sex.

"Once we do it, I always enjoy it, but if I have too much sex in one week, it's like my vagina unravels. It turns into a loose scarf."

I was relieved to hear this intel. No one tells us these things! I'd stopped having sex with my ex-husband a year or two before we parted ways, and I wondered, if we'd kept having sex, would we still be married? It had become both physically and emotionally uncomfortable. Years of tallied-up wrongs had accrued, and while make-up sex is a thing, I'd never met anyone for whom resentment sex holds any appeal.

"It's been twenty-two years since I've been naked with anyone who wasn't my husband, schvitzing next to me in a sauna, or giving me a pap smear," I said. "And the idea of unfamiliar penis?" I shuddered. "I'm not sure I can do it. Maybe familiar penis would be less traumatizing."

Jill suggested that we locate an old boyfriend willing to be my starter penis. I mentally scrolled through the list of old lovers who weren't married, weren't gay, were aboveground, and whose last names I could remember. I told her that my best bet was Brad. I'd made out with Brad at my bat mitzvah, and we had a fling in the summer before heading off to college. Thirty years later he showed up at one of my book tour stops. In a hotel lobby in St. Louis, he'd announced that he was still carrying a torch for me.

There was definite chemistry and I almost invited him up to my room, but he had on acid-washed mom jeans and he told me that he and his wife had an open marriage. I'm not sure which was the greater turn-off, but I think it was the latter because if I was going to have sex outside of my marriage, I wanted it to be illicit.

"You are *so* getting on a plane to St. Louis."

It says a lot about where I am in my life that I felt compelled to ask, "Do people fly places to have sex?" Jill looked at me like I'd questioned whether or not the earth revolves around the sun.

"That's why people get on planes. Half of the passengers at every airport are flying somewhere to have sex!"

Jill, now my canoodling coach, ordered me to get into shape. "Do you have a vibrator?" she asked.

I described the sad array of artifacts in my sock drawer, including an antiquated bullet-shaped device powered by a separate battery pack, the sex toy equivalent of a cell phone the size of a shoe. During the course of my marriage, the wiring to the battery pack had loosened. Mid-flagrante I'd twist and turn it, like a divining rod, hoping to spark it back to life. Alas, in the end, the connection proved tenuous; then, like the marriage, it flatlined.

"You need to get ready for St. Louis. Here's what you're going to do. You're going to get yourself a brand-new vibrator. You're going to use it twice a day. *This is your job now.*"

Jill spoke with such authority that I drove straight over to the Pleasure Chest. It had been years since I'd been inside the adult entertainment emporium. The choices were overwhelming and otherworldly. Row after row of blindingly bright-colored phalluses were displayed on what seemed like city block–long shelving. I grabbed the first one I saw: the purple one. Like Prince! Only it was more Barney purple than Prince purple. But fuck it, so to speak, or literally, because the one next to it was a lurid blue. *Blue's Clues* blue. The next was red. Elmo red. It was a veritable Crayola box of dildos, and in what might represent a unique partnership between Silicon Valley and Silicone Valley—a.k.a. the San Fernando Valley, just a few miles north and known as the capitol of porn and silicone accoutrements—the display included smart devices, whose apps allow you to turn on your sex toy remotely. "Siri: turn the heat up to *sexy time*, put on my Sade mix, and get that vibrator whirring, mama's on her way home!" I resisted the temptation to purchase Silicon Valley's silicone because I was certain I would become a news item: "Spinster Stimulated to Death by Hacked Vibrator." *Her sister warned her if she didn't start dating it would end poorly, but she wouldn't listen!*

Back in my car, I ripped open the packaging and discovered that my Purple One had a USB cord. I plugged it into the car phone charger so I could commence my training regimen as soon as I arrived home, except the cord was so short that I couldn't conceal it under the seat. I prayed I wouldn't get pulled over by the police. Not only would it be mortifying to be seen shuttling my purple passenger, but technically, I was driving while armed. After all, a penis is the most dangerous weapon in the world.

In the privacy of my boudoir, I considered my trainer, auspiciously named the Wave. Is there anything more reassuring than being greeted with a wave? Still, I hesitated. I'd mentioned to Jill that penetrative sex was uncomfortable, and she'd suggested that it was due to the sad state of my marriage. "Uncomfortable" was my euphemism for "excruciatingly painful." This is a taboo subject, one that I was loath to acknowledge to Jill and even to myself.

Have you ever fallen off of a motorcycle traveling at a high speed, skidded across the road, had your skin peeled back and gravel embedded in the raw tissue? Me neither, but this aptly describes menopausal intercourse.

As women cease menstruating, the body's estrogen levels wane.

Younger women who've undergone chemotherapy often experience similarly decreased hormonal production. In practical terms, you've got one of those micro-purses and the only thing you can fit inside is a lipstick.

If a woman continues to be sexually active throughout menopause, her chances of maintaining healthily elastic vaginal tissue are more likely, proving that old adage, "use it or lose it," annoyingly accurate. Despite the fact that 45 percent of women in menopause report experiencing discomfort during intercourse, you will find no real cultural conversations depicting the kind of grimacing discomfort I've experienced.

Someone in the medical establishment named this condition vaginal atrophy. It could have been termed "vaginal dysfunction," placing it on par with the neutral-sounding "erectile dysfunction," but no, we've been saddled with the word "atrophy," as though our pussies need to be outfitted with a LifeAlert™ because they've fallen and they can't get up. The name itself makes you want to throw yourself from a cliff, or brain someone with one of those jade eggs that Goop was peddling as vaginal "toners" before the California Food, Drug, and Medical Device Task Force fined them $145,000 for deceptive advertising.*

Erectile dysfunction, on the other hand, as common a malady for middle-aged men, has been normalized to an extent that it's doubtful that there are any adults in the western world who aren't

---

* You can still purchase them on Goop. No longer advertised as toners, they are still sold in the "between the sheets" portal, and it's likely everyone thinks they are intended as such. What else would you do with a black jade egg "between the sheets," rub the creases from your bed linens with it?

familiar with Viagra and Cialis. These phosphodiesterase-5 (PDE5) inhibitors are both routine punch lines to jokes in PG-rated movies and are prescribed for treating impotence. Fear not, dudes who need an erection booster, Big Pharma has you covered. Products marketed to treat ED are advertised on billboards, in commercials, and even on public transportation. A venerated celebrity like Michael Douglas can concede to needing it to keep up with his wife, admitting, "Wonderful enhancements have happened in the last few years—Viagra, Cialis—that can make us all feel younger," in an interview with AARP, yet he still manages to have a story line that includes a romantic interest in his Emmy Award–winning TV series *The Kominsky Method.*

The medical-industrial complex supports even the working not-quite-stiff's desire to extend his libidinous years. ED has FDA approval and an official CPT code, which means that some insurance plans cover it, while even more men receive reimbursement through physicians using a diagnosis code related to urinary incontinence. Off-brand substitutes are available on the interweb for as little as seventy cents per little blue pill. For women experiencing sexual dysfunction, no such luck. There are no clever billboard ads, no confounding two-bathtub Cialis commercials. Not even Real Housewife of Beverly Hills Lisa Rinna, who once gamely walked the red carpet at the Emmys wearing Poise brand bladder leakage padding under her gown, has dared mention the drought down there.

During my marriage, I attempted to address the problem, first by applying natural remedies: elixirs made from olive oil, avocado, and honey, ingredients that make a tasty salad dressing but did nothing to make intercourse tolerable. Next, I tried topical estrogen creams, which are supposed to encourage the production of natural lubrication, trusting in my gynecologist's assessment that these treatments contain such low dosages that they wouldn't increase my estrogen levels more than the HRT (hormone replacement therapy) I was already doing.

The issue of the safety of HRT is a clusterfuck of contradictory information. It's widely accepted that HRT is contraindicated for women with a history of breast cancer, especially estrogen-receptive breast cancer, or the BRCA1 or BRCA2 gene, but for the rest of us, it's every woman for herself. On the day I started HRT, *The New York Times* published research supporting the link between HRT and increased risk of cancer. That same day, *The Wall Street Journal* published a study that came to the opposite conclusion. What's undeniable is that there is less testing on medications that are solely developed for women. You might as well flip a coin.

You could say that I went with tails. I tried an estrogen suppository that felt like I was sloshing around town in wet bikini bottoms. Next was a hormone delivery "ring," something akin to a diaphragm. I was at my coworking space when I noticed a pungent smell. I assumed someone had ordered a fermented dish from our local vegan eatery, but I was mistaken. My crotch smelled like kimchi. Not only did I not experience any relief, but these therapies are also short-acting, so I had to apply them frequently even as the chances of having sex were diminishing. I gave up. The Miele twenty-four-inch, stainless steel washing machine with temperature consistency, powerful heater, and load control became the primary focus of my fantasies.

But this was prior to my visit to the Pleasure Chest. Surely, the Wave could revive me. The instruction manual described it as "surging in a come-hither motion," but after a brief tour of my interior, I was sure that the Wave was digging a tunnel from my uterus to Palm Springs. The smooth silicone exterior was even more chafing than an old-fashioned plastic model. It felt like sandpaper against my skin.

I put a pin in St. Louis and once again shelved the whole enterprise. That is, until the night that I bumped into an old acquaintance at a charity benefit, an empty nester whose wife had died a few years prior. We'd never slept together, but he was a known quantity. When we hugged, a jolt of sexual electricity ran up and down my spine. We made dinner plans. I wasn't looking for a relationship yet, but dinner might lead to another dinner, which might lead to a nightcap, which might lead to doing my part to lessen the Great American Sex Drought. Suddenly, I was motivated to moisturize and decided to research "vaginal rejuvenation."

I have more than a handful of intimate female friendships, but none had ever mentioned it. I needed to widen the circle to get firsthand info on what sounded like a facelift for your pussy.

I was chatting up three women at a barbeque when I intuited that the alcohol I'd consumed and the relative anonymity of our acquaintance might provide the right lubrication for such a discussion. It worked. All three disclosed that they'd rehabbed their vaginas. Let's call one of them Sage, because she was tanned, toned, had feathers braided in her hair, and was barefoot. Not as in she entered the house wearing shoes and was now barefoot; she showed up to a party barefoot. She's the kind of free-spirited, disposable-incomed person you tend to run into at parties in Los Angeles. Sage had done it on a whim while accompanying a girlfriend to her appointment. Another claimed to have only had the procedure because after giving birth to three children, her doctor told her it would help with urinary continence. The third, a licensed sex therapist, divulged that it had improved her sex life and then tried to rope me into purchasing one of those Goopy toning eggs, which she sells on her website as well.

None of this seemed like a ringing endorsement for vaginal rejuvenation. But over the next few days, I queried my inner circle of friends and found I'd been mistaken. Several of my closest girlfriends had done this procedure, but none had ever spoken about it to any of their friends. What in God's name was this thing anyway?

I learned that the procedure utilizes radiofrequency energy to heat the vaginal tissue. Supposedly, the irritation caused by the laser stimulates "plumping" collagen production. This is the same technology used in laser resurfacing cosmetic treatments marketed under trade names like Thermage and Fraxel, making it *exactly* like getting a facelift *down there.*

Of the several models on the market, my gynecologist offered the Mona Lisa Touch. What's more unsettling, I wondered: pharmaceutical companies hijacking the mystery of Mona Lisa's smile, or that I was seriously considering getting Touched?

Despite FDA warnings about the potential dangers, I called my doctor to schedule an appointment. A series of three treatments was recommended to ensure the best results, and I should expect to need maintenance boosters each year. For the rest of my sexually active life. The cost? $2,500. Because of the absence of FDA approval, there was zero possibility of insurance coverage, even though, just like Viagra and Cialis, doctors recommend the lasers to treat female urinary continence. I'd hoped to one day remodel my kitchen; instead, I had my vagina reupholstered.

The treatment was scheduled to take place at a fertility clinic in Beverly Hills. Only a few months earlier, I'd accompanied my kid to this very same clinic. Ezra needed some testing relating to their congenital anomalies, but the receptionist assumed that we were a couple trying to conceive. "Good luck," she'd said, to the mortification of my child, and squeezed my arm. The fertility clinic was flooded with light and orchid flowers the size of beach balls. Couples and entire families were relaxing on long banquettes. On this visit, I was sent to the waiting area designated for the vaginal rejuvenation clientele: a vestibule with recessed lighting, high wingback chairs, and black-and-white photographs of snowy peaks and sand dunes on the walls. On the day of my first treatment, the only other client had on dark glasses and a sun hat with a wide brim. Like me, she had shown up solo. Twinsies.

I was ushered into the clinic's outpatient surgical center and assumed the standard gynecological exam position while a numbing cream was applied. Imagine readying a chicken for rotisserie cooking, only I was the chicken. If only I'd been rotating around the wand, that might have been more entertaining. Instead, it felt like Gordon Ramsay was whipping up a panna cotta in my uterus. When the laser was applied to my labia, it had that same prickliness of swiping your scalp with a curling iron. Thankfully, the entire procedure took less than thirty minutes. I left with an ice pack lodged in my panties and instructions to wait four days before test-driving my renewed and improved nether region.

In spite of the ice pack, it felt like my pussy had been nuked. On the way back to my car, waddling and bowlegged, the outer edges were on fire, and the inside was pulsating. It was practically humming with energy and might have been visibly glowing through my jeans. I tried to recall what it reminded me of—something I'd just heard about on the news? Then it hit me. That day, the first images ever captured of a black hole were published. Disk shaped, super heated, with a vibrating, gaseous center? I'd turned my vagina into Pōwehi, as it was named, for the Hawaiian word that means "dark source of unending creation."

Four days later, I was scheduled to go on my third date with my "gentleman caller," as I'd taken to referring to him. My sister, the self-appointed cruise director of my sex life, put me on notice. "Third date? You're going to need to put out." While we'd had a lot of laughs, I wasn't certain there was a third-date "pants off" rule, but I decided to ready myself, setting the clock, like the countdown to a NASA launch.

I left my office earlier than usual, slathered my limbs with creams and lotions, did a last-minute vacuuming of cat hair, and corralled the stash of tweezers I hide around my house, the telltale signs of a middle-aged bearded cat lady. At T minus two hours, I realized I'd neglected to get even one of the lubricants friends had endorsed. I raced over to the local health food store, but I'd forgotten my reading glasses.

"Hi, can you help me?" I said to the clerk, pointing in the direction of the personal care items. "Which of these can be applied to the inside of my vagina."

"Can't you come back later with your glasses?"

"There's no time! I might have sex in two hours!"

He begrudgingly read the labels out loud. There was a butter that provided soothing moisture for your lips, skin, and "other places." Another claimed to be an "intimate" balm. The language was coded and neither of us could tell if they were intended for internal or external use, so I purchased one of every product that cost under twenty dollars.

It was T minus forty-five minutes when I dashed home. I placed the astonishing array of lubricants on the nightstand next to the bed. Viewing my collection of bottles, tubes, and tins, it would be natural to assume I was a doomsday prepper for lubes. It was a small comfort that after the big earthquake hit and the inevitable lubepocalypse ensued, I could sell them from the trunk of my car and make a fortune.

I put on an ensemble from Lingerie Box.

Houston, we had liftoff. To return to the purse metaphor, my clutch is sleek but spacious enough to fit the essentials. Between the Mona Lisa, the lingerie, and the cornucopia of lubricants, it cost $2,780.86 to become sexually active again. A lot has been made of the continued wage gap between male and female workers, but in reality, that's nothing compared to the sex gap. When you figure in the cost of his little blue pills, I'll have to have sex 556 times to bring us to parity. My gentleman caller kindly offered to help amortize the cost downwards. I took him up on the proposal.

Dear Girlfriends

Dear Michelle, Claudia, Patricia, Stephanie, Jen, Donna, Neena, and Jyoti,

You know how we've read about girlfriends buying tiny houses in a bestie row and how we've always said we should do that? This is that email to say: we should do that!

We'll save money by downsizing and we'll be together! For those of us that are still married—Jen and Donna—I'm throwing salt over my shoulder as I write this, but we've all read actuarial tables, right? What better time than now to plan for our future?

Email me back if you're in and no hard feelings if not, you can still be in the book club and I'll love you forever.

Hoping to grow older with my favorite people in the world—scratch that, get older—growing anything at this age makes me think of things like a goiter.

xo Annabelle

—

Dear Michelle, Claudia, Patricia, Donna, Neena, and Jyoti,

I heard back from most of you and there were some questions.
First of all, yes, tiny houses do have bathrooms. They have tiny
bathrooms. I'll look into pricing out a tiny spa, say, something with
a sauna and Jacuzzi?

Michelle asked about the fact that most tiny houses have bedrooms accessed by ladders. Well, that's our incentive to stay in shape.
We'll talk about long-term health insurance later. Meanwhile, na-
maste ladies, keep doing those downward-facing dogs!

Oh, Jen emailed to say that Kenny has such great genes that
he's going to outlive everyone. Can we all agree that his jokes are
beyond dad jokes and sometimes just *no*? So let's keep the plan on
the q.t. for now with Jen, because we've all witnessed Kenny's code-
pendent relationship with fatty meats—the issue might resolve itself.

I left Steph off the chain, because she signed her last email with
"blessings, sister goddess Stephanie." This is not going to be a coven
or goddess colony.

best friends forever, Annabelle

—

Dear Michelle, Patricia, Donna, and Neena,

Updates: Jyoti is out. She says that after three months in lockdown she doesn't think she's a good candidate for a tiny house. I
tried to explain that *that's the point*, we'll be so close to each other
that should we ever need to quarantine, we can chat from our tiny
windows, but she just doesn't get it.

Also, I've taken Claudia off our list. You know how Claudia said "Okie dokie artichokie" a lot on our day trip to Joshua Tree National Park? That's going to get old.

I found a tiny house spa—it's a got a large wooden Jacuzzi and a sauna but it was pricey, so unless we use them to double as a washing machine and dryer, which sounds a little too pioneer woman, I think we should nix this idea.

Next steps: I think we can all agree that it's not a bad idea that we send any accommodations for special needs and disclose any health issues so we can't say we didn't know what we were signing up for, right? There's nothing you can reveal that would be prohibitive, so let's be transparent.

Also, we need to pick a location. Give me an idea of your ideal part of the country and let's see how close we can get to that.

grateful for our sisterhood, Annabelle

—

Dear Michelle and Patricia,

Wow, I did not know that Neena had fibromyalgia. Thank goodness she's got it under control, but that's a lot to take on, right? Honestly, I'm not even sure that's really a thing. Is that like Epstein-Barr? Did that turn out to be real? What's the latest research on that? Anyhoo . . .

Donna is out. She said that the accommodation list I sent was annoying because I wrote a category of preferred milks and "cashew nut milk was one nut milk too far." Fun fact: cashew milk has fewer carbs than oat milk and takes less water to produce than almond. Tiny houses have tiny storage spaces, so doesn't it make sense to share staples? Anyway, we're going to need to be super accepting and I'm not sure her comment was offered in the spirit of our community. Also, she hums when she cooks, which I read might be a sign of early-onset dementia.

Here's the scoop on the geographic preferences:

Michelle's daughter is in college in Chicago and she plans to settle there, and she's got siblings in both Portland and Seattle, so she'd like to stay sort of midwesty to Pacific Northwest. Also, Michelle's son has been living with her since he graduated from college and might never leave, so she's up for getting a second tiny house for him and I'm cool with that because it'll be good to have someone to keep us up to date on new music, and he has a side hustle (or maybe it's his main hustle?!) baking edibles, kk?

Patricia's brother is in Long Island, her kids are in Brooklyn, she loves her GP in the city, and she's got a sister in Connecticut—they aren't speaking so I guess that doesn't factor into it—but Patty really, really wants to stay close to the tristate area so she can make pilgrimages to the Shake Shack on Eighth Ave. and Forty-fourth.

My kid plans to come back to Los Angeles after college and my sister will probably wind up in the Bay Area with her kids, so it's best for me to be somewhere near California, although I might need to get a second tiny house like Michelle. Wait—we'll tell our kids they need to bunk together—who knows, maybe they'll fall in love and it'll be one of those "we met cute" stories?

Two possible homesteads:

I found a restored old western town for sale, it's eighteen acres and a white elephant so the price is good. The setup has a bordello, a saloon that seats forty (perfect for family gatherings), a jail, a church, a teepee, and a train caboose. The only problem is that it's in the high desert in California and with climate change it could be problematic. Plus, it might be a bit geared toward people into cosplay, that's not really our generation, right?

There's also a large property available in the Ozarks. The Ozarks has the lowest cost of living in the U.S. and we can get gorgeous lakeside property for a fraction of what it would cost anywhere else. I'm sure when you google you'll see that the Ozark Mountains are home to a bloodsucking parasite that the American Heart Association says causes diseases associated with heart failure, stroke, or life-threatening ventricular arrhythmia, and Missouri has dangerously high radon poisoning levels, but it takes twenty-five years of exposure to do any damage, so I think we're golden. I'm crossing my fingers that you'll agree that this central location will allow us to travel back and forth with equally shared inconvenience.

I guess we need to ask one more time if anyone has underlying health conditions that we didn't mention earlier, and also, what's the status of your health insurance, pension plan, and your investment asset allocations? (I recently moved my paltry savings out of the stock market and am totally in bonds, whew!)

I'm so touched and honored that we're throwing in our lots together, Annabelle

—

M.,

It looks like it's just us chickens. Patricia emailed, "I spent my whole fucking life trying to get out of the butt-fuck backwoods and I'm not fucking going back." I guess that mid-Atlantic accent of hers was all bullshit. I always suspected that, LOL.

Is it OK if I start listing you as my emergency contact? OMG, we're really doing this!

xoxoxo, A.

—

Dear Michelle,

I have to admit that I was a bit surprised that you sent my recent blood work results (forwarded per your request, assuming confidentiality) to your internist. I *am* borderline diabetic, but that's not the same thing as having it, that's why it's called borderline.

And I don't have long-term insurance and maybe I should have mentioned that earlier, and it's true that I lost quite a bit in the stock market before I reallocated and maybe I should have mentioned that earlier too, and I don't want to be presumptuous, but I sent your modest investment portfolio to my friend Jackie who is really good with this stuff and she feels your exposure is a bit on the risky side and it might be time for you to go more conservative. Just sayin'.

Anyway, I hope we can move forward and put aside any concerns. You know, we're the only ones who ever finish the whole book in our club, so it's really fitting that we'll be in our tiny houses together. I never say "the universe is working things out for us," but maybe it is?

lurv ya like a sister, Annabelle

(note: my ex-boyfriend Howard who is an attorney is cc'ed on this email)

—

Dear Capitol Lenders Reverse Mortgage Brokerage,

I am currently reviewing my financial planning and I'd like to explore the option of a reverse mortgage. I have heard this whole scheme is a boondoggle that always backfires and winds up bankrupting the borrower, so don't bother giving me the sell, just send me the deets.

thank you,

Annabelle Gurwitch

You're Doing All the Right Things, Everything Is Going to Work Out

"You're doing all the right things, everything is going to work out."

I'd been repeating this over and over, like a mantra, to Ezra in the summer before their sophomore year of college. I said it not because I believed it, but because I was one hundred percent convinced that the opposite was true, although I'm not sure which of us I was trying to convince.

It was a miracle that Ezra had made it through the first year of college. Actually, it was a miracle of modern science that they'd made it through the first year of life. If Ezra had been born twenty years earlier, their quality of life would have been severely affected; sixty years prior, children born with the constellation of birth defects referred to by the acronym VACTERL rarely survived.*

---

* Birth defects associated with VACTERL include vertebral, anal, cardiac, tracheal, esophageal, renal, and limb anomalies. At one point, they had both a feeding tube and a colostomy bag. Ezra's little body looked like a grade school science project.

During their first five years of life, Ezra underwent surgeries to repair the anomalies associated with the syndrome, whose cause remains unknown. To see Ezra's sunflower of a face and early athletic prowess, you wouldn't have suspected their ongoing health issues. A well-meaning person sent me a copy of *Don't Sweat the Small Stuff.* "Thanks so much," I said, but what I wanted to say was "Kindly fuck off."

In the looking-glass world of children with birth defects, instead of bonding at Baby and Me classes, we spent our days at doctors' offices. One of our regular stops was the office of Dr. Elaine Kamil, who'd been monitoring Ezra's kidney since their birth. On one occasion, we were awaiting test results when my heart started pounding. I had a sudden onset of vertigo. Like Jell-O sliding down a wall, I slumped onto the waiting room floor. I didn't know it, but I was having a panic attack. Luckily, I had a babysitter with us, and I sent Ezra home with her in a cab. Dr. Kamil ushered me into her office, gave me a banana, rubbed my back like I was an infant, and sent me home with a cherry lollipop and good news: Ezra's kidney was doing double duty, compensating for the missing one.

The next morning, I went to see a chiropractor. "Can you recommend a calming natural supplement?" I stammered, explaining that I'd been up most of the previous night sorting through medical bills. (Within the first year of Ezra's life, we'd racked up over $400,000 in bills; if we hadn't had our union health plan, we'd have been bankrupted.) I'd also developed a twitch in one eye. The chiropractor kicked me to the curb. "Screw that, you need to get on something stronger than anything I can give you." I went on SSRIs. It helped.

Looking back on the impact Ezra's medical odyssey had on my

life, it's unfathomable to comprehend how profoundly Ezra was affected. Doctors once assumed that babies didn't retain the memory of trauma, but it's widely accepted now that preverbal experiences have lasting effects. Given the constant prodding and poking, and the sometimes unreliable adolescent body (there are still days when some of the bodily functions most of us take for granted simply don't cooperate), it's no wonder that Ezra tried to manage their frustrations with alcohol, cannabis, and other drugs.

In every family, there's always one parent pushing for greater intervention, and in this family it was me. One of my favorite ways to avoid work is to take on unwieldy home projects, like cleaning the gutters or culling the herd of decommissioned stuffed animals. I challenge the claims that weed doesn't destroy brain cells, even just a few, because that's the only explanation for why Ezra would hide drug paraphernalia in the same places over and over. Half a dozen times, I found weed pipes in the gutters, rolling paper in Paddington Bear's boots, and bongs fashioned out of reusable water bottles. That last one really hurt, because whenever they'd asked for another reusable water bottle, I'd congratulated myself on instilling earth-friendly values.

Things came to a head the day I saw Ezra hiding a backpack in the shrubbery outside of our home. A backpack in a bush is an invitation for a mother to look inside. It contained film canisters stuffed with weed. I'm embarrassed to admit that my first thought was, *How quaint that some conventions never go out of style: kids still hide pot in film canisters.* There was also a stash of plastic baggies, the internationally recognized sign for "I'm dealing drugs." I was holding the backpack when Ezra returned to retrieve it. "Oh, Mom, that weed? It's Zoe's," Ezra said and casually took out their phone and began texting someone as I stood there in disbelief. My cell phone dinged. I read the incoming text out loud. "Oh shit, Zoe, my mom found my weed, I'm so fucked, baby."

That was when I discovered that my avatar icon on Ezra's phone was a magnifying glass and my spouse's was a cat.

"Why am I the magnifying glass? I want to be the cat!"

"Mom, you're always micromanaging me. Dad's fun."

The most "fun" I could come up with was to offer every kind of therapy Ezra would agree to, some I could afford and others I couldn't but spent money on anyway. Cognitive behavioral therapy, talk therapy, berating by a parent—which isn't actually a form of therapy or even all that helpful, but I did it anyway. Standing in the home drug testing kit aisle at the CVS, I'd wonder if the tests that cost forty-seven dollars were any better than the seven-dollar ones. Sometimes I bought the cheapest ones; sometimes the most expensive. Ezra tested negative when they were obviously impaired and tested positive when they seemed sober; there didn't seem to be any discernible pattern to the results. Years later, Ezra explained that they'd cheated on all of the tests. Those stories of people hiding someone else's urine in a bottle in their pants' pockets? Those are not apocryphal. I wish I'd known that then because I could have dumped buckets of money from my car window and at least made some passersby happy.

Friends were draining their IRAs by sending their kids to wilderness recovery programs and rehabs that cost 40k a week. I tried to find creative solutions that cost less than a Hamptons beach house. I arranged for Ezra to volunteer one day a week at the Children's Ranch, a local nonprofit that offers therapeutic services for children with learning, social/emotional, and developmental challenges in the form of caring for horses, rabbits, and other small animals. Ezra assisted the instructors with the younger children. A year in, Ezra asked me, "Mom, am I a volunteer or a client?" I hadn't thought about it before. "Both?"*

I'D WAKE UP AT FOUR in the morning, wondering if I'd left some stone unturned. There was always some specialist just beyond my reach. On the assumption that they were self-medicating with drugs, I tried to score an appointment with a doctor known as "the medication whisperer" in Los Angeles. I was warned that you had to know someone who knew someone who was already a patient, sacrifice a virgin in a volcano, and even then, you might have to wait six months to get evaluated. It was also $950 for the initial consultation. I didn't have access to any of those things, but I lost several hours to googling "how much can you get for a healthy middle-aged kidney?" all the while knowing that selling a kidney wasn't even an option, because my kid might need me to donate mine one day. Ezra briefly saw another doctor who diagnosed them with ADD, but the drug trial was short-lived once we learned Ezra had given the Adderall to their friends.

Ezra was having trouble completing assignments and staying organized and on task, things that can be symptoms of ADD or ADHD or some other combination of letters, but there was also a chicken-and-egg question. Were they self-medicating to deal with

---

* The director of the Ranch explained to me that the caretaking offered a model of self-soothing to the kids, and it did feel like an oasis of calm, but it wasn't enough intervention for Ezra at that point.

learning and processing issues, or was the drug use causing learning and processing issues? Or both? Who wouldn't have difficulties if you were in a classroom with fifty other students?

Ezra had thrived at a public middle school with a tight-knit community and small class sizes. They'd played upright bass in the orchestra and jazz band, but high school at one of the most well-thought-of institutions in the city didn't pan out. With the large class sizes, an hour-long commute, and witnessing a gang-related stabbing on campus, things went sour quickly.

I cobbled together a team of tutors and homework coaches. I put up calendar whiteboards only to have Ezra cover the dates with penises and Jabba the Hutt smoking a hookah, impressively drawn with a Sharpie. In a last-ditch effort to shore up plummeting grades, I hired Lacey, a highly recommended time management specialist. Lacey bounded into our lives with an indefatigable can-do attitude. Like an executive-function Mary Poppins, she produced folders, note cards, spreadsheets, Post-its, and color-coded filing systems out of her magic carpetbag and set up a homework station in the dining room. For the first few weeks her eyes sparkled with enthusiasm, but after two months of facing Ezra's impenetrable wall of attitude, she had a thousand-yard stare. She limped out of our lives, and Ezra transferred to a fledgling charter school, Valley International Prep, acronym VIP, which I took to calling the Island of Misfit Toys.

At the Island, someone was always sulking in the hallway, sobbing about their love life or some other drama—and that was just the instructors. The students were each uniquely blessed with neuroses I'd never heard of, like the moon-faced fawn who carried a prescription horsehair brush to gnaw on instead of chewing on her own hair. The entire enterprise was a well-intended hot mess.

Instructors fled like rats from a sinking ship and the curriculum shifted from week to week to reflect the gaps in the teaching staff. One of the school's selling points was that the kids would prepare their own lunches under the direction of a professional chef. This was intended to be a self-esteem and self-reliance building activity, the only problem being that the administration neglected to prepare the kitchen for inspection. It was condemned by the city health department, and each day, the entire student body lined up at a single vending machine at lunchtime. We'd been told that the empty lot adjacent to the school would be cleared to serve as the PE field; well into Ezra's second year, it was still derelict. I assumed the role of campus janitorial staff. Armed with garbage bags from home, I cleaned the grounds and even the lot, but PE never made it onto the schedule.*

Throughout the day, I'd see the principal hobbling to and fro like a battle-weary soldier, mumbling that it was a terrible mistake to have started the school. One day, when I politely inquired if the vice principal might refrain from greeting Ezra with the salutation "Hey Stoner," she told me that we were welcome to transfer to another school. She added she was rooting for my kid because they had potential. "Not like these other Valley trash." I never complained again, but I did recruit a cadre of professional writers to help the "other Valley trash" with their college essays.

Unlike *Survivor,* you couldn't get voted off this island. There was

---

* In Los Angeles, you can always tell what kind of neighborhood you're in by the billboards. Alongside Buckley, an expensive private school, Balenciaga sneakers and Tom Ford sunglasses; en route to the Island, bail bonds and Teeth in a Day dental implant outlets.

nowhere else to go, unless a family had unlimited resources. Los Angeles private academies geared toward students with learning issues have aspirational names like Fusion, Futures, and Avalon and cost over $50,000 per year, if they'll even accept your child. One friend's daughter, adopted from the foster system and several grade levels behind her peers, was considered too much of a challenge for those schools. Her options were limited to two even pricier choices. "We're trying for Soar, and if that doesn't work, we'll tour a new place that's opening up, called Tree," my friend said. "Tree? What's after that? Soil? Sand? Sediment?" I asked. "Nope, after that, you're homeschooling," she sighed.

I hit my lowest point at Ezra's senior year annual appointment with Dr. Kamil. We'd formed a close bond by then and had regular conversations not only about Ezra's health, but about Elaine's children. When Ezra started drinking heavily, I felt it was important to share this information, and Elaine, in turn, shared about her son Adam's struggles with addiction. After Adam died from a drug overdose, I asked Elaine if we might talk about Adam's death with Ezra, reasoning that hearing the consequences of drug use (Ezra had yet to have friends overdose), from someone who'd been a part of their life for only one hour less than I had, might have an impact. During that appointment, Ezra defended drug use and neglected to offer even a modicum of compassion to Elaine. If there was ever a time I wanted to put my kid for sale on eBay, that was it. (Ezra has since made amends.)

I'd suggested that Ezra take a gap year before applying to college, even though *The New York Times* reported that the gap year was a "growing and expensive trend," with parents expected to design a character-building experience that might cost more than a year's college tuition. I wasn't anxious to spend even more money than tuition, but I worried about the drinking and drug culture on college campuses and wasn't sure Ezra would even gain acceptance anywhere.

It's a testament to Ezra's tenacity that the high-wire act of self-medicating, home drug testing, therapy interventions, tutoring, and even Lacey's short tenure allowed them to pull off high test scores, well-executed essays, and getting into their first choice of colleges.*

During the winter of that first year away from home, their drug and alcohol use spiraled out of control. Pictures on social media (since taken down) invariably showed Ezra in various states of intoxication. Every time I saw a photograph, I imagined those cartoon "drunk bubbles" circling their head. Ezra hit bottom, went cold turkey, and insisted on white-knuckling it until they could finish out the semester. They returned home and entered an I.O.P., an intensive outpatient recovery program for the summer.

Ezra's peers at the treatment center were wrestling with many of the issues plaguing this generation, everything from game addiction, substance abuse, eating disorders, and body dysmorphia to generalized anxiety.

The treatment program included forming a supportive community. Parents were required to attend feedback sessions during which we offered feedback, with guidance from the counselors, on each other's progress. During these sessions, on the drives to the sessions,

---

* I was committed to sending Ezra to public schools on principle but also because of the expense, but the slow trickle of money diverted to all the interventions to make public school work probably cost almost as much as private school tuition.

and really, every other minute of my day, I wondered if I could have done something that would have resulted in a different outcome.

One of the parenting choices I'd felt was unimpeachable was my attempt to give Ezra a taste of the free-range childhood I'd enjoyed. We were renting a modest house located at the summit of a narrow hilly street when I was pregnant. I rarely saw our neighbors, and was convinced that Hill People, as I referred to them, with their homes hidden behind high walls and gated driveways (ours was one of the only houses without one), weren't as friendly as Flats People, at the base of the hills, with their wide sidewalks and welcoming front porches.

Our hill neighbors were doing renovations that stretched on for more than two years. They never managed more than a brief wave and a "We're so sorry for all the noise, we'll leave you a bottle of wine!" before roaring through the massive entrance gates to their massive estate. That bottle of wine never materialized.

My intuition proved correct. Purchasing the Widow McGarry's house bought us more than just a home, we'd gained a neighborhood. Flats People were friendlier. We had annual holiday parties, attended family weddings and funerals, and neighbors rallied with visits and errand running when someone fell ill. Ezra attended grade school with "the Kids Across the Street," as we called them, carpooling every day and playing together after school. The Kids were a bit older, and eventually everyone went their own way, but we had halcyon years. During a family session, I looked across the circle and realized the familiar-looking couple and their son, the faces I hadn't been able to place, were our old hill neighbors. Hill People, Flats People, we'd ended up in the same place. Would our lives have turned out differently if we'd never moved? Impossible to know, but I didn't mention that to them, as it seemed inappropriate to say "Hey, you owe us a bottle of wine" at a rehab.

By the end of the summer, Ezra announced they were ready to head back to college. The director of the outpatient treatment center suggested Ezra put in a bit more time with them, but my kid was determined. I'd observed growth and maturity over the summer, but I still worried. Ezra confided to fearing that they'd fried a substantial number of their brain cells. There was no foolproof assurance of their readiness to relaunch. It was going to require a leap of faith I couldn't muster, but I came up with an eleventh-hour plan: a zombie escape room.

I'd never done an escape room, but I'd read articles describing them as a kind of immersive game play. Escape rooms were being touted as the future of psychometric assessment tools, replacing the Myers-Briggs test. Corporations were using them to encourage cooperation and team-building skills, and friends claimed they were family bonding experiences. My understanding was that teams entered a themed room and were "locked" inside and tasked to find hidden clues, strategize and delegate tasks, and reason through challenging puzzles, allowing for an "escape." In cities across the United States, escape rooms were becoming so popular that there were waiting lists to be locked into the steerage section of Viking ships, Mayan pyramids, bank vaults, and *Phantom of the Opera*–haunted theater backstages.

Zombie stories are my favorite dystopian genre. Zombiism seems like an awfully good metaphor for motherhood. Once you've got it, your life as you knew it is over and you're destined to spend the rest of your days under its spell. I'm also a sucker for *The Walking Dead*. Maybe it's because Andrew Lincoln, who portrayed Rick for ten seasons as the leader of a new society, was so adorable, he made the end of humanity seem bearable, even desirable. Would Ezra assume a leadership role, like Rick, and spearhead our release? Or maybe they'd be like Glenn, Rick's trusty and steadfast lieutenant. Following orders, without the glory of leadership, might even portend better as an indicator of maturity. Any of these scenarios offered a chance to hang back in the crowd and observe Ezra's coping skills in a stressful situation. What higher pressure could there be than trying to escape the undead? I signed us up for a zombie-themed escape room on the night before their flight back to school.

It was only when we arrived at the escape room that we discovered I'd mistakenly signed us up to play the game alone. "OMG Mom, this is a metaphor for my childhood," Ezra complained, but before they could make a break for it, our wrangler shoved white lab coats at us and said, "There's been an outbreak of a zombiism. You are society's last hope. You 'scientists' have exactly one hour to find a cure." She ushered us into a cramped windowless room, our "laboratory." The door slammed shut and the lock clicked into place.

It was all a bit hokey: HELP! was scrawled across a wall in bright red paint and a bloodied plastic hand and foot rested on a hospital gurney. Like Ezra, I too have anxiety, and I can easily spiral into catastrophic thinking, and something about that click set me off. The first clue to finding a cure for zombiism involved an equation. It was simple algebra, something lik 6 x ? = 36, a problem that any adult could solve except me, because numbers and symbols paired together make me panic. My heart raced as I realized I had signed us up for an hour of solving math problems. "We're all going to die," I screamed.

"Mom, it's just us. Jesus. I got this," Ezra snarled, making best efforts to preserve team cohesion. They solved the equation, followed the trail of clues, and methodically dispatched one puzzle after another while I paced in circles, muttering, "Oh my God, oh my God, oh my God." "Get a grip, Ma." Ezra took hold of my shoulders and steadied me. I was incapable of completing even the simplest of tasks, a kind of game of Operation. We were to hand crank electricity and then pass a wire through an electrified hoop. I couldn't stop shaking long enough to carry it out. Some clues required pattern recognition, but we were not provided paper and pencils, so memorizing sequences of numbers was required. I was a useless meat puppet, but Ezra's brain was firing on all cylinders. I assumed our escape would involve forming alliances, just like in *The Walking Dead*, but it was a blur of math and science. I was capable of solving only one problem on my own. With a rainbow selection of colored liquids in front of us, I was charged with combining two vials of liquid into a tincture that would be purple in hue. "Red and blue make purple," I chanted gleefully and repeatedly, ecstatic to be channeling a mastery of kindergarten-level science knowledge.

Suddenly, zombies were banging on the outside of the lab door. A video monitor in our room flickered on and in the most amateurish produced footage ever produced within Hollywood city limits, escape room staffers swayed and moaned.* I recognized our wran-

---

* I knew they were staffers because the "zombies" hadn't bothered to put on costumes; they wore the same college T-shirts that I'd seen staffers running the other games wearing.

gler by the timbre of her moan as she pounded on the door. Even her banging had the air of "they're not paying me enough to put more muscle into this," but the element of surprise was effective. The final component to the antidote required a set of skills that once threatened to derail my college aspirations.

In my senior year of high school, I was earning a D in chemistry due to my refusal to memorize the periodic table. I begged my teacher to award me a C minus, explaining that to do otherwise would result in the loss of my spot at NYU, where I'd already been accepted. "I'm going to be an actress and I will never need to use the periodic table." Now, the future of the world depended on my knowledge of the periodic table! The banging on the door was getting louder when my kid, whose brain cells had not all evaporated, correctly identified Bh as Bohrium, a radioactive isotope. The door clicked open. Not only was the zombie apocalypse averted, my kid had coped with my panic attack in a locked, windowless room. Ezra would be returning to campus.

That night, I slept the deep sleep of a parent who felt secure about their kid's future. Ezra had managed to save the world *and* keep a cool head while their mother was freaking out. Really, what better sign of maturity was there than handling a panicked parent? I'd never achieved anything close to that in my entire lifetime.

The next morning my ex-husband and I convened for the drive to the airport. "You're doing all the right things, everything is going to work out," I repeated, and this time I meant it.

We were standing outside of the blocked-off area, watching our child approach the TSA checkpoint, when dogs started barking, lights flashed, sirens blared, and Ezra was escorted away. This is how we learned that they'd gone to a late-night bonfire rave and hadn't showered or changed clothes and were covered head to toe with traces of accelerant. Ezra was questioned and searched, but ultimately identified as one of the throngs of college-bound students on their way back to campus, and cleared to travel. Ezra had remained calm in a stressful situation, again.

I was angling to catch a glimpse of Ezra as they ascended the escalator when a line from the John Cassavetes film *Love Streams* popped into my head. Gena Rowlands says, "Love is a stream, it's continuous, it never stops." I pictured the umbilical cord, that stupid feeding tube, and a river of love connecting us. It felt like waves of love were gushing out of me and rushing toward them. But a river flows in only one direction. My kid wasn't looking back at me. They were facing forward, toward their future. At some point, our children ride the current of love away from us. And that's the way it's supposed to be. If we're lucky, and we do all the right things, the best we can hope for is to be ignored by our offspring.

Free to Be . . .
They and Them

IN THE FALL OF 2018, I was attending a writers' conference in Manhattan. Most of the attendees were women around my age, and as the evening wore on, the subject turned to the use of the pronoun "they" by gender-nonconforming individuals. Everyone was supportive in principle, but found "they" confounding from a grammatical standpoint.

I took the opportunity to describe how I'd recently attended a book signing for multimedia artist, LGBTQ+ activist, and queer scholar Zachary Drucker. "Zachary is really pushing the envelope. She's a trans woman who has kept her birth name. If this becomes the norm, this could really upend implicit gender bias. *They* is just the tip of the iceberg," I said with the kind of bossy-pants stridency I tend to channel when defending ideals with which I don't have personal experience.

The subject of pronouns was only vaguely on my radar. I'd read about University of Michigan student Grant Strobl's successful petition to be addressed by his professors as His Majesty. Mr. Strobl is the national chairman of Young Americans for Freedom, an organization that places pop-up anti-abortion "graveyards" on campuses, so addressing him as His Menace seemed more appropriate, but no one had asked me. Strobl's petition was an act of protest but it was precedent-setting. Not long after the Strobl case, my friend Bernard, a professor at a progressive arts college who always knows what's brewing in the zeitgeist, even in the most nascent stages, described the brave new gender identity frontier from his vantage point.

"At the beginning of each semester, everyone introduces themselves with their pronouns. I have students who identify as female but present as male, present as male but identify as female, and one student who comes to class dressed like a pirate. Sometimes I think they're just fucking with me."

I asked him how he, an openly gay man, would have identified had he been queried in college in the late 1990s. "I wouldn't have known what they were talking about. Identify?" He paused and added, "Italian!"

The morning after I grandstanded with the grammar police, Ezra and I met for lunch at Grand Central Station. Over soup, Ezra mentioned that a new roommate, Berber, an art student, was moving into their dorm suite.

"Great! What's her/his given name?" I asked, picturing Berber's parents lamenting the time and energy they'd expended on picking out a name only to have their kid change it to a moniker that evokes densely woven carpeting.

"Berber's pronouns are they, them, and theirs, and it's not only a carpet, Mom, the Berbers are also a people, a marginalized people, and I would never reveal Berber's deadname."

"'Deadname?' What does that mean?" I asked. Ezra explained that the term refers to addressing someone by the name they were given prior to transitioning or identifying as a different gender. "Isn't that a bit dramatic? Couldn't they just retire the name, like they do with numbers on sports teams?"

Not only was this a glib and insensitive retort, I'd failed to intuit where the conversation was heading. It was then that Ezra informed me that they also felt most comfortable identifying as nonbinary and that "they" would now be their pronoun. It was all so easy when it was speculative.

Although I claim to be unconditionally supportive of my child, I suspected that this was, to use the phrase my mother invoked to describe many of my choices, "just a phase."

Many of my childhood memories include my mother rolling her eyes and mouthing "it's just a phase" to my father or anyone else who happened to be nearby. By seventeen, I'd adopted a life philosophy that began and ended with "What would Patti Smith do?" Her tangled hair and wrinkled slip on the cover of *Easter* were my version of a little black dress. It wasn't only a fashion choice; it was an early attempt to identify as an artist and distance myself from a set of values I associated with the twinset sweaters my mother would have preferred me to wear. "Do you have to look like you've been fed through a document shredder?" my mother chided, adding that my appearance was an embarrassment to our family. The answer was "yes" then and it is "yes" now. It was never "just a phase."

Even more importantly, I'd entertained this "phase" notion despite having considered myself an ally long before the term "ally" came into vogue. Much of my adult life was steeped in queer culture.

A theater nerd since grade school, I'd found my twin of sorts in

Brian. We'd both been bitten by the drama bug early on and were paired off until we graduated high school. We'd fallen in love in *The Fantasticks*, married in *Fiddler*, and married again in *Our Town*. Both sets of parents had joked that there would be fewer guests at our real-life wedding than had witnessed our betrothals on stage. We knew better. For almost as many years as we'd known each other, I was his beard, first at school dances and later at gay nightclubs.

In New York, my next stop after the dorm at NYU was an apartment in the Meatpacking District, the center of the leather bar scene in the West Village. It was a short walk from my place to the Pyramid Club and Danceteria, where RuPaul and Madonna often shared the same cabaret bills as a band I performed with that featured John Sex, a singer known for his bleached-blond pompadour, pet python, and appearing in a diaper. Given that I slapped most of the makeup available in the tristate area onto my face and used as much Aquanet as the drag queens I was performing alongside could spare, many in the audience assumed I was also in drag.

I aspired to the kind of envelope-pushing work being created by artists like queer solo performer and activist John Fleck, one of the NEA Four, the group of artists whose (minuscule) grants from the National Endowment for the Arts were rescinded after being labeled dangerous and degenerate by the Reagan administration. It remains a life goal to have my work labeled dangerous and degenerate.

Many of my liaisons fell into a category that can best be summed up and delivered with a shrug: "It was the eighties." There was the dancer who'd realized he was gay while serving in the navy, a boyfriend who did housework in frilly aprons, and another—not a performer—who had nonetheless amassed an extensive collection of dresses and wigs. "Does my wearing dresses bother you?" he'd asked. "Not if you look good in them!" I'd answered.

When my closest friends were diagnosed with the disease that had yet to be named but was being called "the gay flu," my time was split between work and caring for friends. Days pursuing work as an actress were punctuated with doctors' appointments, followed by rotating all-night shifts tending the needs of the feverish friends who were disappearing before our eyes.

Queer identity was never "just a phase": not for Brian, nor any of the friends, my chosen family, that I loved and lost to AIDS.

Ironically, and completely by chance, the house I purchased from the Widow McGarry is located directly across the street from John Fleck's home. I was delighted that my kid would need to look no further than John or his partner Randy for terrific role models.*

This being my worldview, I vowed not to influence my child's choices, but I did once beg Ezra to let me braid their shoulder-length hair into Pippi Longstocking pigtails, and I ponied up five dollars for that privilege.

During their adolescence, I marveled at this generation's fluidity. It was delightful to see male and female friends comfortably displaying affection, holding hands, and co-sleeping, minus the kind of macho performative male posturing I'd witnessed in boys when I was growing up.

---

* After I told John and Randy about my impending divorce, they invited me to join the Gay Outdoors. That's their weekly hiking group composed of gay men whose average age is "old enough to remember the leather bars of the West Village." I am the sole female and only straight person enjoying the gay outdoors on Mondays, 6:00 to 8:00 p.m., on our local hiking trails. It's been a welcome homecoming.

When I first introduced Ezra's new pronouns into conversations, a few family friends asked, "How did this all start? Did you notice any symptoms?" Like they'd come down with a nasty flu.

"Well, there was that time when they asked me to buy them combat boots and fishnet stockings," I replied, which was true, but unrelated to my child's gender identity.

It also confused some people into thinking I had more children than I do, allowing me to indulge in some dad humor: "Well, it often feels like I have more than one child!"

I can only wonder at the amount of resolve that must be summoned to transition or identify as a gender different from the one you were assigned at birth. With some religious groups still devoted to "praying the gay away" and trans rights under attack in many countries around the world (including our own), I harbor not-unwarranted fears for their safe passage through the world, but my initial dismissiveness disappoints me.

"I respect Ezra and all these young 'uns, and I will call them anything they want to call themselves. I hope they can be patient with us dinosaurs who are having a hard time adjusting. 'He' and 'she' have been our identifiers for thousands of years," Fleck confided in me the other day.

Two years later, I take misgendering seriously, but I still slip up. The English language has irritating limitations. Particularly vexing is the lack of words referring to your offspring that don't have associations with small children. I shared this frustration with Morgan Walsh, an actress and founder of Gender Nation, a nonprofit that donates LGBTQ+ affirming storybooks to public schools. Her kids are younger than Ezra, but she foresees introducing them with "a playful phrase like 'this is the full-grown human who still needs me for grocery money' or 'have you met my grown child who can legally operate an automobile, but probably shouldn't.'"

How long before it's commonplace to use pronouns "that need not necessarily reveal the mysteries of (a person's) underpants," as former GLAAD president Jenny Boylan put it in her *New York Times* column titled "That's What Ze Said"? It seems like we haven't quite reached that tipping point. In 2018, the Pew Research Center found that 35 percent of Gen Z say they personally know someone who uses gender-neutral pronouns like "they" and "them," as compared to a quarter of millennials, while only 16 and 12 percent of Gen X and baby boomers know someone who doesn't use "he" or "she."

In other parts of the globe, change is happening at a faster pace. To date, the UK has rejected appeals for a gender-neutral designation on passports, but you can get that in other countries, including Argentina, where young people are aiming to transform Spanish into a gender-neutral language.* With Merriam-Webster choosing "they" as its word of the year in 2019, it appears that they is here to stay.

As always, the next generation pushes the envelope and they're changing the culture, beyond the expected coastal urban centers. My friend Elizabeth, who lives in a small town in North Carolina, told me that when Syd, "the gender-creative individual who sprung from her loins," now twenty-two, came out as bisexual and went to the high school prom with their girlfriend, she and her husband bought them matching boutonnieres. In college, Syd identified as

---

* Countries where you can choose X on your passport include Canada, Germany, Australia, Denmark, and India. California allows residents that choice on their driver's license.

queer, but now is a nonbinary lesbian. "Syd's in their room right now, building a shrine to Persephone," Beth said on the phone the other day. "As long as they're happy."*

What do I do when someone asks, "So how does this nonbinary thing work? Do they date boys or girls or something in between?" This might be the one instance where "don't ask, don't tell," applies. "Humans" is my preferred answer. "Beautiful humans in baggy clothes."

One refreshing attribute of the "young adult who often goes over their usage plan on their phone, incurring extra costs" is that they, like many in their generation, eschew buying new clothes, including anything with a designer label, and for that matter anything new, other than tech. Ezra shops only secondhand stores, a laudably thrifty attribute. When "the biped who is graduating college soon and coming back to live under my roof" needs something, we make pilgrimages to our favorite resale shop, Housing Works, the New York City–based nonprofit whose proceeds support both people living with AIDS and the housing insecure. On the day Ezra announced their pronoun change, the store was packed, so we shared a dressing room. I was down to my full-body Spanx and they were trying on an adult onesie large enough to double as a sleeping bag. I handed them a Members Only–style jacket. "Mom, check my drip," Ezra said as they modeled it (Gen Z speak for "check out my outfit"). "How did you know I'd like it?" White with aquamarine and hot pink stripes, it was made of that swishy material favored by

---

* Gender identification and sexual identity are two different but related subjects. I am including examples of my experiences here because they both occupy space in the ever-changing landscape of queer culture.

octogenarian golfers. With its blend of polyester and nylon, it's like the vinyl siding of athleisure.

"I picked out the ugliest thing I could find," I explained. Ezra grinned. I'm just another ordinary cisgender heterosexual, but I suppose it was inevitable that my offspring and I would wind up sharing a dressing room at Housing Works.

As to the future? We'd probably do well to look to groups like Nameberry, which track popular baby names, as prognosticators. Pamela Redmond, the author best known for her bestselling book *Younger* and a cofounder of Nameberry, writes that we can look forward to watching gaggles of Rebels, Justices, Wrens, Rivers, and Skyes grow up. As evidence of gender-fluid naming gaining in popularity, she cites a surprisingly large number of girls being named Ezra. I hope so, because they might one day identify differently, and I put a lot of effort into picking that name. But should they decide it no longer fits, any annoyance on my part will be a passing phase. To borrow from the album that provided the soundtrack to my childhood, it is my most fervent hope that all beautiful humans are *Free to Be . . . They and Them.*

You're Leaving When?

A TWENTY-FIRST BIRTHDAY IS CONSIDERED a milestone in many cultures, often celebrated with "I'm finally legal" drunken revelries. I doubted that Ezra, with three years of sobriety, would throw a kegger, but hoping to be included in the festivities, I'd finagled a teaching gig near their campus on the East Coast. This would be Ezra's first birthday party I'd be attending that I hadn't organized. A milestone for me, as well.

As the train sped north up the Hudson River from Manhattan, I had two and a half hours to prepare myself. Since the college drop-off, three years earlier, I always seemed to be saying the wrong thing, doing the wrong thing, glancing with questionable intention—even the sound of my breathing might be deemed overtly aggressive. Ezra could navigate the internet with ninja-like dexterity but sometimes seemed as helpless as a baby chick. Was I supposed to be a mama bird, chewing food for her fledging nestling, or a mama bat, who nudges her pups, with sink-or-swim dispatch, out of the roost?

Having grown up at the intersection of laissez-faire and benign neglect, by the time I was in high school, my comings and goings garnered little to none of my parents' attention. "Eighteen and out" was the expectation. Kim, another mom friend, put it more bluntly. "My mama read us the riot act: 'Don't any of y'all come home, unless it's in a box.' And none of the four of us did."

Many of us tail-end boomers and Gen X were lucky enough to come of age when rents were affordable and employment was available with relative ease, making striking out on your own challenging but not impossible. Enlisting parents' assistance in everyday matters was unthinkable. Long-distance calls were expensive and, in my family, to be made only in an emergency. "Mom, I've grown a second head" *might* have merited a long-distance call. Chances are I wouldn't have reached them because they didn't have an answering machine.* With our Wi-Fi umbilical cords tethering us to our young, parenthood in the digital age is a zero-sum game.

When our kids graduated high school together, I'd cried into my friend Susan's shoulder. "There are so many books about raising your kids, but no one teaches you how to let go."

"Don't sweat it," said Susan, who has two older children, "They're not going anywhere."

I'd worried that Ezra might not be ready for college when they'd asked to bring a comfort animal with them. I assumed they meant our cat, but I was mistaken. Ezra hoped to get their friend Cam-

---

* Life prior to answering machines seems to refer to a time when dinosaurs walked the earth. I guess I am one of those dinosaurs.

eron (who wasn't college bound) designated as an emotional support animal. Since the mid-aughts, universities have expanded the categories of comfort animals to include bunnies, chickens, snakes, and even horses, but to date, no humans have been approved.

Then, on our drive to the campus, my perfectly imperfect kid blurted out, "Mom, am I a failure?"

"Why on earth would you say that?" I said, heartbroken to hear them give voice to so much anxiety at such a landmark moment.

Ezra had been scrolling through social media and learned that the iconic musician and producer Frank Ocean had invited a high school buddy to record with him. Ezra's Soundcloud and Bandcamp postings hadn't attracted Ocean's attention and they were crestfallen, convinced that the window had already closed on their future prospects. They seemed to lack that annoying adolescent braggadocio, that biologically hardwired over-confidence that allows young people to take big chances for better or worse. Now that your internet presence trails you like toilet paper stuck to your shoe, the time-honored prospect of a fresh start after high school seems murkier than in the past.

On my first day of college, I felt like I was granted reprieve from all past embarrassments. No one would know about that unfortunate double perm!* A clean slate. Before the close of that week, I'd dyed my hair jet black, dropped five pounds, acquired a New York accent, and voila, I'd created an entirely new persona. Of course, that wasn't true, but I didn't know that then.

During the hustle and bustle of outfitting the dorm room, I dismissed my concerns. As our unpacking wound down, I hugged

---

* Nora Ephron coined the term "unfortunate perm" and it can't be topped.

Ezra. "You do not want to be that person whose glory days were in high school. The worst thing that can happen in life is to peak early." Tears were shed (mine), and Ezra promptly shoved me out the door.

For approximately ten minutes I entertained a dangerous notion, a phrase that history has taught us to be wary of "Mission accomplished." Then a text arrived. "Mom, can you put money in my account, my meal plan isn't loading." Should I have replied, "You figure it out"? Maybe. But baby bird needed sustenance!

On a daily basis I receive texts that range from, "PLZZZZ SND $ for Flamin Hot Cheetos" to "I have a headache, do you think I might have a brain tumor?" Thankfully, that was only a fleeting but worrisome anxiety. I don't answer every text, but that's mostly because I can never remember to charge my phone.

My kid knows how to push my buttons. The morning after the 2016 election, I awoke to a flurry of texts.

"What's up?"

"Mom, I spent my allowance, but I want to go to a protest rally."

"Are you kidding me?" I replied. "You expect me to underwrite protesting an election you forgot to vote in? No fucking way."

"But Mom . . . someone I *like* is going."

I'm constitutionally incapable of standing in the way of social justice, even as an excuse to hook up. Resistance was futile.

"Do you think I'm edging into helicopter territory?" I'd asked my friend Chris.

"Well, you didn't allow them to experience the consequences of their actions." That's her definition for helicoptering. Chris has drawn lines in the sand that I haven't managed to stick to. With a daughter profoundly affected by autism and a son studying engineering at Purdue, she understands the need both to be available and to set boundaries. She gave me a cautionary example of what she thinks of as too much involvement, sometimes called "snow-plow parenting," an entry she'd seen on a Purdue parents' message board:

> My son has a lab that ends at 11:30 AM in X building and then a class at 11:45 at Y building. How will he make it? I have scoured all the bus schedules and I walked the distance myself—it is cutting it close. Does anyone have an idea of how to handle this?

I'd never tracked the grades or courses Ezra was taking, much less the routes to get to classrooms. Was I too hands-off?

Those interminable winter and summer college breaks were particularly stupefying. Weeks prior to their arrival, I'd excitedly text "When are you arriving?" but less than twenty-four hours in, I'd already be asking, "You're leaving when?"

Three years into Ezra's college career, they'd already spent more time under my roof than I'd logged with my parents during my entire life after leaving home.* So I fell back on that time-honored trope of Jewish motherhood: food equals love. Call it Remembrance of Breakfasts Past.

A hearty first meal of the day seemed especially important while Ezra attended the Island of Misfit Toys. Each morning, I'd prepared a full meal—or warm buttered toast, at least—missing a day

---

* On visits home, my mother hung a sampler she needlepointed herself on my bedroom door. It read, "You are leaving Sunday?" But I was determined to do better!

only if I was working on the road. I really hit my breakfast stride on the weekends. I'd wake up to find teenagers sleeping about the house in piles, like a pride of lions. Better my home than elsewhere, I figured. Like an all-day breakfast diner, I'd crank out heaping piles of eggs, French toast, matzoh brei—the Jewish Hamburger Helper of egg dishes. The most reliable way to get teenagers to recognize your existence, make eye contact, grunt in your direction, or even, sometimes, engage in conversation is when shoveling food onto their plate.

These meals also provided essential intel. It was on one such occasion that I learned that Ezra had been sharing his Adderall (during that brief, unproductive stint on medication). I was serving up a frittata as Ezra's friend Lucas filled me in on his post–high school plans. Lucas was talking at an unintelligibly rapid pace, blinking and licking his lips repeatedly, while pushing food around his plate.

"Lucas, are you high?"

"Why, yes, Ezra's mom, I am."

"Honey, what are you on?"

"Ezra's ADD medication."

That was some good intel. I hoped that re-upping this routine might pave the way for connection. Instead, Ezra slouched through the front door and devolved into a single-cell amoeba. Each reentry period seemed like what I'd read about astronauts returning from long stretches in zero gravity, how they lose so much muscle mass that they have to learn to walk again. Ezra napped, watched cartoons, left dirty laundry strewn about the house, and snuck cereal into their bedroom. In anticipation of their arrival, I stocked up on their favorite food, only to learn that I was behind the curve.

"Almond milk? I don't drink that anymore. Why didn't you get oat milk?"

"Oat milk? No one drinks oat milk anymore; can you please get hemp?"

"Why isn't there any turkey meat in the fridge?"

"Why is there so much turkey meat in the fridge?"

I tried to keep up. "But you said you were vegan … But you said you weren't vegan anymore … You know what? If you want something, just go to the market yourself!"

I called my friend Aparna, a family therapist, to ask if this warranted intervention.

"Your child is imago."

"What is that, and is it contagious?" I asked, thinking it sounded a bit too much like lumbago.

"When a caterpillar cocoons, before it transforms into a butterfly, it's in an in-between, formless state. It's called imago. That's your child when they first leave the nest—something in between a child and an adult," Aparna explained.

"How long will this go on?"

She advised me to lower my expectations and pick one arena where I could be unconditionally supportive during their time at home. "Does bathing count?" I asked.

On the other hand, there were signs of burgeoning maturity. During sophomore year, Ezra phoned with news: they wanted to transfer from one liberal arts college to an even more liberal liberal arts college. They announced this intention with the words every parent longs to hear: "Mom, I want to go freakier."

"Go for it," I replied. "Let me know how it turns out." I was certain they'd never manage without assistance, but Ezra proved me wrong, even brokering a generous financial aid package.

They'd founded a sobriety club on campus, were sharing a rented house that they'd furnished themselves, managing a challenging course load, and had worked their way up from dishwasher to line cook at the local pub, but visits on their new turf were confounding. Once, I was treated to a delicious salad bowl they'd prepared at the bar, but when we went back to their house, it was bone-chilling cold. "I don't know what to do, Mom, the landlord hasn't turned on the heat." Mounted on the wall, directly above the living room sofa, was an old-fashioned analogue thermostat. Ezra and their roommates thought it was some kind of kitschy antique fixture left over from another century (which technically it was) and had been freezing for a month.

On a recent stopover, Ezra asked if I wanted to hear a new composition. In middle and high school, Ezra had played the upright bass. I never tired of hearing renditions of "Fly Me to the Moon" or a Bach cantata. Since then, they had moved on to experimental electronic compositions, all of which I'd titled "My Migraine."

The tracks, Ezra explained, were a mash-up of ambient, trance, night core, dubstep, deconstructed club, drone, and distorted low-fi psychedelia. What does that sound like? Darth Vader played at half speed, Alvin and the Chipmunks played at warp speed, whale callings, and the cries of one million babies whose diapers need changing.

The last thing I wanted to do was appear less than supportive, so I summoned ye olde acting skills, honed during the career I'd aged out of, to affect a neutral facial expression for my rapt audience of one.

"Do you think it's good?" they asked.

"The world will let you know."

This is really the best of all possible answers because the only sure sign that something won't become the next big thing is if your mother likes it.

I felt both privileged and mystified by Ezra's desire for my approval. I'd never sought my parents' opinions of my artistic pursuits. Was it my kid or was it a whole generation that seemed to be individuating at a snail's pace? Was I becoming one of those curmudgeonly "What's the matter with kids today" kind of old fogies?

I called Kathryn Bowers, whose daughter is about the same age as Ezra. Kathryn coauthored *Wildhood*, a book that looks at coming of age in a variety of species. I asked if she felt our offspring deserved being labeled "special snowflakes," that derogatory term often invoked by older boomers that implies feeling entitled to special treatment.

Bowers explained that every adolescent, whether hummingbird or high schooler, has a unique experience of this volatile and vulnerable phase of life. A universal feature of it is intense social pressure and an obsession with where they fit into the group. For birds, mammals, and even crustaceans, social hierarchies are formed during adolescence, and "the labels they pick up" during this first sorting follow them for the rest of their lives. For hyenas, for example, adolescence is when a cackle (that's the fabulously evocative nomenclature for a grouping of hyenas) "battles for social rank," which determines who gets the best food and most desirable mates. Higher-ranking hyenas even get more sleep because they don't have to work the night watch shift. Scientists call this sorting in the hierarchy "status."* "Once status is fixed, the lower-status hyena, although not as privileged as the alpha, can find happiness as an essential member of the cackle. Our kids' childhoods have been disrupted in many ways that can make them seem less fully formed— but one of the most profound is social media. Our kids don't get a break from the assessing and the comparing to others; they're continually jangled, up and down. It's physically and emotionally draining and debilitating." Bowers considers the digital era as much of a disruption as coming of age in the Industrial Revolution.

That rang true to me. One of Ezra's closest friends in college woke up one day to find that he'd been "canceled" overnight. Social media postings calling him a Nazi, because he frequently wore camouflage outfits and had a buzz cut, meant that he was shunned on campus. This kid was a gentle giant, and also Jewish. He'd been so devastated that he'd transferred schools. He was only one of numerous young people we know who've experienced cancel culture.

The stakes are so much higher for our kids in every arena. Growing up, I'd managed to waste a lot of time wondering if the Professor and Mary Ann would ever make it off Gilligan's Island, but our kids are waiting for climate change to turn Tulsa into beachfront property. This eco-anxiety, as it's being called, is just another in the laundry list of distractions: internet-addled attention spans, school shootings, and the daunting prospect of earning a living in the gig economy at a time when class mobility is the lowest it's been in a hundred years. It's no wonder that along with being labeled snow-

---

* Remember Facebook's status updates? That feature was retired, but the likes and thumbs-ups persist—that's all status sorting.

flakes, Gen Z has also been called Generation Anxiety. As parents, we don't want our kids to fall through the cracks. Hence the tendency to overcompensate.

Ironically, many of our challenges are strikingly similar to those facing our children. In economically stressful times, the populations most vulnerable are those just starting out and those nearing retirement. Gen X once had the reputation of being overly sensitive, spoiled middle children, a generation of Jans complaining that "Marcia, Marcia, Marcia" got all the attention. Only recently has media coverage of our sandwich generation's financial instability confirmed how justified we were in our worries.* As far as redemptions go, this is what used to be called a "booby prize." This makes us empathically well suited to be their parents while at the same time horrifyingly close to their experiences, too matchy-matchy.

Bowers suggests we take a lesson from the animal kingdom where benchmarks for coming of age don't happen on fixed timetables. In lean times, hyenas avail themselves of "extended parental care," continuing to receive food and shelter at home. In flush times, they're more likely to head out earlier. If we allowed ourselves to realign our expectations to accommodate a more elastic adolescence, there would be advantages for our children. The adolescent brain has evolved to be maximally adaptable, allowing for ease in acquiring new skills, which can set them up to be better aligned with new modes of employment and societal structures.

---

* In 2019, the Harris Poll reported that Gen X has the distinction of holding not only the most debt in the U.S., but the most student debt. Many of us still owe money on our college loans and have borrowed for our children's college tuitions. Meanwhile, on average, the cost of college for Gen Z is 150 percent more than for boomers.

I'm all for it. According to sociologist Erik Erikson, who coined the term "extended adolescence," twenty-five is the new eighteen. I'm just hoping that I haven't peaked early because I'm going to need to learn new skills to afford my child's extended adolescence.*

An hour out from their college station, I texted, "Looking forward to the big birthday!" and started doing deep breathing exercises. If our children are in extended adolescence, then where does that leave us as parents?

A London School of Economics study conducted in seventeen European countries indicated that adult children individuating later is such a shocking disruption to parents' quality of life and well-being that, as much as people love their offspring, "the negative impact is similar to suffering an age-related disability such as losing the ability to walk or get dressed." We need a new model of parenting, preferably one that doesn't involve losing a limb.

Even more startling is that many of our adult children enjoy spending time with us. In 2019, NPR interviewed Jacob Ostheimer, a twenty-four-year-old who lives with his wife and mother and stepfather, at a popular karaoke spot in Mission Viejo, California. Ostheimer said, "I'm here right now getting drunk with my mom. The whole family's here."

I'd never done karaoke with my kid, and we wouldn't be getting drunk together, but I was graduating into a different stage of motherhood. I was an imago too. What form was I going to take when I

---

* It's probably time to retire the labeling of our kids as "snowflakes." New research debunks the commonly accepted idea that every snowflake is unique. There are thirty-two basic categories of snowflakes, which is good news, because feeling so unique can be a burden.

emerged? I might turn out to be a butterfly, but moths also cocoon. It could go either way. Just for today, I decided to be a passenger-seat parent.

Ezra and a friend pulled up at the local train station. The car's heat blasting, Billie Eilish blaring, the energy upbeat.*

More of Ezra's posse joined us at the local bowling alley for a late-afternoon match. We played under nicknames inspired by woodland creatures: squirrel, possum, moose, rooster, hawk. For reasons I can't recall, I was dubbed Li'l Chicken. Li'l Chicken bowled some surprisingly good frames but ultimately placed dead last. Afterward, we headed to a restaurant nearby and feasted on delicious curries, family style.

As we dug into our main course, with my kid's friends serving as witness, Ezra announced that they wanted to make an amends to me. That's twelve-step lingo to mean a deeply considered acknowledgment of responsibility. During high school, each morning, while I made breakfast, Ezra snuck into my upstairs bedroom closet and lifted cash out of the earthquake emergency bag. This was how they'd funded their drug habit. Ezra wanted to take responsibility and felt badly about stealing the money and keeping this a secret.

I was stunned. Ezra had exploited my terrible aptitude for math and poor organizational skills. Whenever the emergency cash reserves dropped precipitously, I promptly replenished the stash. I assumed either my husband or I had raided it for groceries or gas,

---

* Eilish, despite being one of the most successful young musicians in the current scene and being tapped to write and perform the theme song for the James Bond film *No Time to Die*, still lives at home with her parents.

never once suspecting Ezra. My insistence on future disaster preparedness contributed to a disaster already underway.

Ezra once said they'd made my avatar on their phone a magnifying glass because I micromanaged them and their dad's was a cat because he was fun, but I was so busy making breakfast, I couldn't see what was right in front of me.

A response seemed to be required, but what? I'd forgotten to ask Kathryn something that now seemed essential. If graduating high school or college and leaving the nest weren't the rites of passage anymore, what then? Offering an amends? If that wasn't a benchmark, what was?

But how much money had been involved in the emergency cash thefts? Had their friends known about the stealing and still eaten my breakfasts? What inspired Ezra to make this amends? Was this curry dairy based and going to give me gas later?

Li'l Chicken had so many questions.

Just this once, as much as I wanted answers, I decided to put down the magnifying glass and be the cat.

"Thank you, Ezra," I said, and I picked up the check.

Ezra and friends turned their attention to videos from Ezra's birthday party the previous night. From what I could tell, it was a raucous event with loud music and numerous cakes thrown in Ezra's face.

With all of our challenges, I'd never allowed myself the luxury of imagining Ezra's twenty-first birthday. My child was surrounded by beautiful creatures of indeterminate gender, in baggy, blobby outfits, each one more unflattering than the next, save one holdout in classic preppy chinos and polo shirt (iconoclastically unfunky!). I felt lucky to be included. Witnessing this outpouring of genuine affection and the heartfelt amends was better than any scenario I could have dreamed up.

We were sipping tea when my newly minted twenty-one-year-old tenderly leaned across the table.

"You're leaving when?" Ezra asked—sweetly, but eager to get on with their evening.

"You can take me to the train station now."

We piled into the car. We drove the winding country roads in silence, through a whiteout of snow-covered fields, trees barren, in relief, a stark moonscape. We arrived at the station an hour before the train was scheduled to arrive, but I'd known that when I offered to close out our time together. I darted out of the car, sprinted to the platform, and didn't look back.

In a Muted Zoom No One Can Hear You Scream

THE NIGHT MY WILL TO live crumbled, it was only a week into lockdown.

I was scrolling through social media when I noticed a post from Gia, my daily hiking buddy. She was so confused about the passage of time that she'd prepared Christmas dinner. A photograph showed her family seated at a dining room table with a roasted turkey, Brussels sprouts, and all the fixings. I've celebrated the holiday with her clan since our kids were in kindergarten, and now here I was, home alone, eating tuna straight out of a can.

I'd feared it might come to this: I was becoming Blanche.

As a young person and avid reader, the ruinous downfalls of Emma Bovary and Anna Karenina, those lovelorn heroines of the Western literary canon, held a romanticized appeal. Equally fascinating but utterly terrifying was Blanche Dubois—a precursory example of cancel culture, as I understood it. Tennessee Williams put us on notice. What was the most grievous fate a woman could suffer? Unmarried, financially insecure, beauty fading, unable to cope with her reduced circumstances, and—horror of horrors— dependent on the kindness of strangers. *A Streetcar Named Desire* ends with Blanche unceremoniously carted off to the loony bin.

I'd seen a version of Williams's story play out in my own family. As a young woman hoping to extend her marriageable years, my grandmother Rebecca shaved several years off her age. Becca fancied herself a beauty and earned a reputation in the family for "putting on airs." She went on buying trips to New York for the family dry goods store in Mobile, Alabama, reportedly spending many a happy hour behind the Red Door at Elizabeth Arden's legendary spa on Fifth Avenue. After her older brother (and benefactor) passed, his children unceremoniously cut her off, and she attempted to add those years back to collect Social Security sooner. She lived out the remainder of her life in reduced circumstances in Atlanta. Until her death, Becca carried a blank check, made out to her by her brother, secreted in her bra along with her "mad money," as proof that she'd once been a beloved sister and in hopes that the family might change their minds and she could once again take her rightful place in the community. She never failed to issue reminders to all of us grandchildren to "always stay close to family," even as many of them distanced themselves from her. Chin lifted, body at a three-quarter angle, feet positioned just so, hand on hip, she'd pose for pictures as though a woman of great stature till the end. As an actress, I'd hoped to play Blanche by channeling Becca. I just didn't want to become her.

IN FEBRUARY 2020, I WAS keeping my inner Blanche at bay. All the strategies I'd employed to keep my life buoyant seemed to be working. I had the dream tenant, a college student cramming two years of courses into one; she was either burning the midnight oil at the school's library or at her girlfriend's apartment. I had the perfect amount of mothering in my daily life. The students I volunteered to tutor at the local high school were appreciative and eager for my suggestions, and once our work was completed, I didn't receive texts asking for money, or a laundry list of things I'd done wrong. I never heard from them again. It was ideal. I had my community choir, and when a hot-yoga studio opened up in my neighborhood, I turned it into a bargain-basement day spa. The monthly fee amortized to less than twenty dollars a class, and on some days I'd take a class and spend another hour schvitzing in the heated room. Ezra was heading toward college graduation and had lined up an internship with an art and performance space in Los Angeles. I'd cobbled together writing assignments and speaking engagements to see me through the summer. My desk in a shared workspace gave me water-cooler camaraderie, and to ease the loneliness of the long winter nights, I was sponsoring open houses for local writers in my living room on a weekly basis. I'd even had a string of promising dates. "No more Miss Havishams!" I exclaimed to Gia, referencing yet another unnerving literary incarnation of spinsterdom.

On March 16, my city went into lockdown.

In a matter of days, my tenant hightailed it home, gigs evaporated, our office was shuttered, school closed, choir furloughed, open houses canceled, and Gia, the mother of five, was unavailable, now running a Little House on the Quarantine, as was the potential beau who'd folded an ex into his household. Ezra sheltered in place with housemates near their campus on the East Coast and I made frantic runs for provisions, stocking up on anti-anxiety medication, coffee, and chocolate, my essential food groups. Untethered to a daily schedule, time seemed to be folding in on itself. I fell behind on writing deadlines. Completing a sentence was a Sisyphean task.

Weeping into my canned tuna, I googled mental health hotlines. In *Streetcar,* a nurse and doctor, whom Blanche mistakes for a gentleman caller, escort her . . . elsewhere. In some stagings, she's led away in a straitjacket. I knew it wasn't an ideal solution during a pandemic, but even a day room in an asylum seemed preferable to solitary confinement at home. I'd thought I'd been through the worst of times, yet things had gotten even worse. I was going full-on Blanche. I had one last bar of sea-salt dark chocolate, which I promptly devoured. Then I had an idea.

In a sugar-fueled manic panic, I fired off an impromptu email to approximately 180 writers to join me for three hours of "writing alone together." Some were close friends who, like my hiking buddy, had young children and, I suspected, might not be available, so I included members of the Invisible Institute, a loose affiliation of nonfiction authors with East Coast and West Coast branches, most of whom I'd never met, and others with even more tenuous connections. To ensure my own commitment to showing up, I requested that folks not RSVP.

Some did anyway. One writer reacted as though I'd admitted to torturing puppies. "What? You want to write alongside other people? I thought you were a write-at-home-alone person, like me. I'd never get anything done! I'm stunned!" Several had pressing obligations: "I'm homeschooling my kids." "On grocery runs for aging parents." "Scouring the Southland for toilet paper." "Sorry, day drinking."

Day 1

I changed out of my night pajamas and into my day pajamas and opened my Zoom session expecting to find dozens of writers stationed at their desks. Five showed up. Four Invisibles, three who'd attended my open houses but with whom I'd had the briefest of exchanges (these were quiet writing sessions), and one I'd never met. The fifth was a Westside comedy writer whom I hadn't seen in months because I live on the east side of town, and as every Angeleno knows, if you live on opposite sides of the La Cienega divide, the avenue separating the two halves of the city, you might as well be residing in different states.

I laid out informal rules of engagement for what I hoped would make for a productive writing session. After chatting for fifteen minutes or so, we'd mute ourselves, write for ninety minutes, break for a chat, and write again for ninety minutes. Fifteen minutes turns out to be an interminable length of time in cyberspace with virtual strangers. We began writing after five minutes.

Westsider kept us entertained with what was, for most of us, our first exposure to that now familiar Zoom green-screen globe hopping. One minute he was writing in front of the Eiffel Tower (OMG!), the next on the Golden Gate Bridge (hilarious!), and finally in a Trader Joe's aisle lined with empty shelves (funny and uncomfortably close to home!).

When I was able to tear myself away from the disastrous way my computer's camera angle made my neck look crepey, I stole glances at the others, delighting in seeing humans other than the cast of *Succession*. Somehow, the herd mentality kicked in—or, given our small number, it might be more accurate to liken the effect to how yawning is contagious. For the first time since locking down, I was able to resist googling "where's Dr. Fauci?" every ten minutes. Reinvigorated by having lengthened my attention span, I dashed off invitations for the next day, adding an additional evening session. As an afterthought, to gin up attendee numbers, I posted links on my social media feeds.

Day 2

Two returning Invisibles and three writers I'd never met—Tampa, Chicago, and another Westsider, who'd seen my invitation on social media—materialized at the appointed time. Dispensing with the chat altogether, we muted ourselves and got to work quickly.

Chicago was seated on a twin bed in a child's bedroom and every so often a sprightly girl, maybe seven, swooped in for a hug and skipped away. This simple interaction elicited what I can only describe as a *Handmaid's Tale* heart-wrenching response. "A child! Do we still have those?" Only a few days into lockdown, my worldview had already warped into an unrecognizable landscape.

Suddenly, I was treated to a close up of Tampa's crotch. *Oh, no, is he going to take his clothes off and masturbate?* I held my breath. What was I thinking inviting strangers? Tampa was merely rising to take a stance at his standing desk, but once situated, my screen showed an even more intimate image. During that first session, I'd been so transfixed by my own stressed-out face that I hadn't noticed: typing into our documents on our computers had the unintended effect of us peering directly into the camera lens.

As the session stretched on, during those dull, aching hours of staring off into the middle distance, the writers' faces registered a kind of blankness that I've only ever seen in dementia patients. Sometimes a quizzical look would pass over someone's features. Only later did I realize that the notes on my office whiteboard were visible behind me: DRY VAGINA, DIVORCE, CAT LADY. Arguably, my Writers Writing Alone Together Zoom had inadvertently fostered a greater intimacy than some sexual encounters. What could be more revealing than witnessing someone wrestling with their own thoughts?

During the evening session, Westsider 1 wrote in the chat, "It feels a little weird having the cameras on, but it's also comforting. I'm sure once I get to know everyone, I'll be even more comfortable."

I didn't have the heart to tell her how much I was hoping not to get to know everyone. In fact, Westsider 2 messaged me with a similar sentiment. She wrote that our time together provided a kind of "safe bubble." The previous day, both she and her husband had been laid off, and it was a relief to be connected with people, but not anyone privy to the news who might ask how she was coping. My daily check-ins with friends and family were essential but were also emotionally fraught reminders of my isolation. This pristine space proved a salve distinct, lifting my spirit like surfing the energy of a crowded street.

Day 3

Awkward. I washed and blow-dried my hair and wrapped a scarf around my neck, but not only was it impossible to look good on

Zoom, I was the only writer to sign on. For a moment, I felt the elation of a grade school snow-day reprieve and was tempted to sign off, but on the chance that someone might turn up, I reprimanded myself: "Go to your Zoom and don't come out until you've accomplished something!" Thankfully, Tampa, another Chicagoan, a newbie from Pasadena, and two Westsiders trickled in. One was a writer who lives in Topanga Canyon, whom I hadn't seen in years, because if you're an Eastsider, visiting someone in canyon country is akin to crossing the continent. The invitation that day included "We'll write like we're at a coffeehouse!" and it galvanized an infectious (apologies) esprit de corps. Topanga, an inveterate café writer, wrote in the chat, "Being able to see your names on the screen means I already knew more about you than I'd know about the people sitting around me in a Starbucks." Before making a bathroom run, Pasadena couldn't resist asking, "Will you be here for a little while? Would you mind watching my stuff?"

Day 4

A strange new normal—signing on, waving hello, and getting to work—set in. I didn't bother with makeup. Tampa, Chicago, Topanga, and two newbies, Brooklynites, who'd heard about us from a friend who'd seen the link on social media. When they signed in, one asked, "What *is* this?" with the baffled expression of someone who's stumbled into the wrong party. But after hearing the brief rundown, they stayed for the entire session and an additional hour, in effect closing the joint down.

That night, I was the lone Zoomer. I sent a text to Ezra, on a whim. "I'm alone, might you join me in my Zoom?" Since college moved online, they seemed to be majoring in Rubik's Cube and minoring in sourdough starter, so I expected they'd be otherwise occupied, but mercifully, Ezra signed on. I didn't mute this session. I wrote accompanied by the gentle click-clacking sound of the cubes sliding into place, as soothing as ASMR. It was only because I'd taken a break and was rapturously gazing at my child, practically a stranger to me now, that I spotted her, the young woman who entered our Zoom and took off the majority of her clothing. Her camera was positioned just below her face, so we'll never know who was more shocked, us at witnessing this striptease together, or our poor Zoom bomber, who'd gone to the trouble of plotting a disruption only to find an audience of two—and a mother and her child, at that.

Day 5

Prior to signing on, I made the mistake of checking my IRA, a huge medical bill landed in my mailbox, and I received official notice that Ezra's graduation ceremony was canceled. David Byrne was to have been the commencement speaker. Also, I'd realized that it wasn't just Zoom making me look unflattering; now that the Botox had fallen out of my face, this was actually how I looked! I wept, more like howled, for several hours straight. If not for the possibility that a Zoomful of strangers was waiting for me, I might still be howling.

"I thought there'd be hundreds of writers," said DTLA, a new addition, upon entering and seeing only six others writing in their own private Idahos.

"Me too. I'm going to mute you now," I said, reveling in the small modicum of control afforded a Zoom host in the midst of worldwide chaos. DTLA warily eyed his screen and he told us that he wasn't sure he would stay, but he wound up writing along with us.

For two hours, Tampa, Maryland, St. Louis, Maine, Chicago, Brooklyn, DTLA, and I enjoyed the intentional anonymity of our intimate vacuum. The last hour it was just Tampa and me. I don't know anything about Tampa, except that he's a librarian who prefers writing at night, but it's possible that during those five days I spent more time with him than I did with my ex during the last year of our marriage.

I've always resisted that phrase "something is everything" because there's always a new something, and if all those somethings are everything then everything is everything, and if everything is everything then everything is meaningless and everything is nothing. It turns out I was wrong. Maybe Blanche was onto something. The kindness of strangers is everything.

When the only thing standing between me and emotional collapse was one last bar of sea-salt dark chocolate, people whose last names, professions, personal aspirations, and political affiliations were unknown to me had rescued this Blanche's sanity.

The grocery store clerks, postal workers, the government employees I hope will push through my unemployment claim, the frontline team who will care for me if I fall ill, the masked strangers—neighbors I just hadn't met yet—who exchange nods and peace signs as we give way to each other on the sidewalk. Even our Zoom bomber gifted us with an unforgettable memory.

We are all potentially Blanches. We are all strangers capable of kindness.

Writers Writing Alone Together persists. Sparsely populated, we write five days a week for three or more hours. Our confederacy is made up of regulars, Westsiders 1 and 2, Chicago, Brooklyn, DTLA, and Pasadena. We've dispensed with greetings and breaks are rare, but when a newbie or an original Zoomer signs in, we wave or stop and catch up, and there's a palpable energy, a quickening, that passes from thumbnail to thumbnail. Sometimes I shake things up. The other day, halfway through our session, I put on a pink wig, just in case someone looked up and needed a laugh. That person turned out to be me.

Buying a new sofa turns out to have been unnecessary. With my all-carb pandemic diet, I am my own couch. Is this what it means to be adaptable? I hope not, because I miss hugs and handshakes. Even though I've eschewed all things French, I miss double cheek-kissing. I even miss phony air-kissing. I miss all the kisses I have yet to give and receive. I miss shoes. And hard pants.

"Welcome stranger, you found us," I type into the chat section every day. "We share this virtual space as needed, so come and go as you like, we're all in this together. Alone." In place of the coasting I once hoped for, I've found community, in a most improbable incarnation. And each time I hit "end meeting for all" I am grateful, both for the virtual company and that in a muted Zoom, no one can hear you scream.

Acknowledgments

EXCERPTS OF SEVERAL ESSAYS IN this book first appeared in shorter form in other publications. "In a Muted Zoom No One Can Hear You Scream" appeared in *Los Angeles Magazine,* thanks to executive editor Maer Roshan and editor Hailey Eber. "You're Doing All the Right Things" appeared in *The New York Times* under the title "Back to School with Narrow Escapes and a Mother's Love," edited by Roberta Zeff, editor extraordinaire. An excerpt of "If You Lived with Me You'd be Home by Now" was published in the *Los Angeles Times* thanks to my editor Susan Brenneman, whose tireless standards have improved my writing over many years. A play based on this story was commissioned by En Garde Arts's Uncommon Voices series and featured in the ALL ARTS streaming series highlighting theater with a social justice theme, produced by Anne Hamburger and Jesse Green and directed by Bart DeLorenzo. The *Los Angeles Times* essay was underwritten with a grant from the Economic Hardship Reporting Project thanks to David Wallis, Alissa Quart, and founder Barbara Ehrenreich. Thanks, Los Angeles Press Club, for recognizing that essay with an award. It is especially gratifying to be recognized in the field of journalism because as an actress, I once appeared in a hot tub with Rodney Dangerfield in a movie.

Thank you, Anne Hamburger and Rafe and Bojangles Jenny, Joanna and Howard Jordan, Marisa Tomei, Judith, Aimee Lee Ball, Sheila, Sandra Tsing Loh, Cathi Hanauer, Kathryn Bowers, Cari Lynn, Kent Black, Julia Sweeney, Claudette Sutherland, Tall Ann, Judith Sandler, Kris Crenwelge, Hope Edelman, Amy Alkon, Meghan Daum, Heather Havrilesky, Carina Chocano, Jenny Allen, Amy Brenneman, Juel Bestrop, Emily Lerner, Janelle Brown, Erica Rothschild, Michelle Joyner, Maggie Rowe and Jim Vallely, Delaune Michel. Thank you to Laura House, *Tiny Victories* podcast producer Laura Swisher, Tonya Pinkins, Andie MacDowell, Heather Winters, Gia Paladino Wise, Eric Reitz, neighbors: Sally, Jerry and Barbara, John and Randy, and the Golden Bridge Choir. Thank you, Devon O'Brien and Tart Night, Tom Sharpe, Max, Lauren, BriKri, Archie and Millie. Bitch Nighters, Kenny Abramowitz, Andie Townhouse and the Zoomers, Women in Media, Larry Dean Harris and Strong Words, the Invisible Institute East and West, and the Suite 8 Writers Collective.

Thank you for allowing me to share your stories: Keyawna Nikole, Jesse Sabol, and Andrew Gutierrez III and Safe Place for Youth. Thank you to Alison Hurst and Rachel Pedowitz for your compassionate leadership.

Thank you to my literary agent, "My strength is time management" Lynn Johnston, for the time and imagination you applied to this book. Thank you, Dan Smetanka, for welcoming me into the wonderful Counterpoint family. Thanks for the continuing support: Maine Media College, Penguin Random House Speakers Bureau, Rancho Mirage Writers Conference, Live Talks LA, Jeannie Ralston and Next Tribe, Warren Bass at *The Wall Street Journal*, Alison Brower at the *Los Angeles Times*, the Jewish Book Council, and Maximum Fun Podcast Network. It's always a highlight to perform with Catherine Burns, Sarah Austen Jenness and the Moth, and the House of SpeakEasy.

Thanks to Bill Maher, producers Naomi Despres and Robert Solerno, and my longtime agent, Bradley "I bought a Subaru for my dog because he doesn't fit in my Porsche" Glenn, Casey Rabin, and the Buchwald Agency.

Thank you to bossy pants Lisa Gurwitch for being the funny one in the family. Thank you, Pushkin, the stallion of cats! Thank you, Ezra Kahn, for adding more joy and tsuris to my life than any one person has a right to hope for, for the pleasure of witnessing the beautiful human you are becoming, and for always reminding me that you never read what I write about you.

ANNABELLE GURWITCH is an actress, activist, and the author of *I See You Made an Effort* (a *New York Times* bestseller and Thurber Prize finalist); *Wherever You Go, There They Are*; *You Say Tomato, I Say Shut Up* (with Jeff Kahn); and *Fired!* (also a Showtime Comedy Special). Gurwitch was the longtime cohost of *Dinner & a Movie* on TBS and a regular commentator on NPR. She's written for *The New Yorker*, *The New York Times*, *Los Angeles Times*, *The Wall Street Journal*, *Los Angeles Magazine*, and *Hadassah Magazine*, among other publications. Her acting credits include *Seinfeld*, *Boston Legal*, *Dexter*, and *Melvin Goes to Dinner*. In 2020, the Los Angeles Press Club recognized her *Los Angeles Times* essay about opening her home to a housing-insecure couple with an excellence in journalism award. This honor was particularly gratifying for her because she once starred in a movie where she appeared in a hot tub with Rodney Dangerfield. She lives in Los Angeles, cohosts *Tiny Victories* on the Maximum Fun podcast network, and is adapting this book for HBO. Find out more at annabellegurwitch.com.